D1545435

Theology Today

GENERAL EDITOR:
EDWARD YARNOLD, S. J.

No. 25

The Theology of Baptism

BY

LORNA BROCKETT, R.S.C.J.

FIDES PUBLISHERS, INC.

NOTRE DAME, INDIANA

Theology Today No. 25
'The Theology of Baptism'
Lorna Brockett

Nihil Obstat:
Jeremiah J. O'Sullivan, D.D.
Censor deputatus
18th December 1970

Imprimatur:
Cornelius Ep. Corcag. & Ross
11th January 1971

SBN 85342 258 3

CONTENTS

PREFACE

Our baptism was the most important moment of our lives. It was then that we gained release from our solidarity with the sinful world and became members of the Church, the body of Christ's redeemed. The life of the risen Christ became ours; with him we became sons and daughters of our heavenly Father, and were filled with his Holy Spirit. God 'delivered us from the dominion of darkness and transferred us to the kingdom of his beloved Son, in whom we have redemption, the forgiveness of sins' (Col 1.13-14).

Yet for most of us this turning-point in our lives took place when we were too young to understand what was going on. This vital sacrament which made us members of the Church was probably celebrated almost in secret, perhaps even shabbily and in haste. Paradoxically, too, more than half the human race, all of whom God wills to save through his Son (1 Tim 2.4-5), have not received this essential sacrament.

Sister Brockett's book, with the wealth of documentation it includes concerning the practice of the early Church, provides the means of resolving these paradoxes.

E.J. Yarnold, S.J.

ACKNOWLEDGEMENTS

The Scripture quotations in this publication are from the Revised Standard Version of the Bible, copyrighted 1946 and 1952 by the Division of Christian Education of the National Council of the Churches of Christ in the U.S.A. and used by kind permission. Quotations from *The Documents of Vatican II* (ed. W.M. Abbott, S.J.) are printed by kind permission of The America Press and Geoffrey Chapman, Ltd., London. Quotations from Theodore of Mopsuestia are given in the translation by A. Mingana in *Woodbrooke Studies* vi (1933), by kind permission of the Woodbrooke Council; those from the *Odes of Solomon* are given according to J. H. Bernard's translation in *Texts and Studies* viii (Cambridge University Press, 1912) by kind permission of the publishers.

ABBREVIATIONS

Dz: H. Denzinger & A. Schönmetzer, *Enchiridion Symbolorum, Definitionum et Declarationum* (33rd edit., Barcelona etc., 1965).

INTRODUCTION

The aim of this book is to present the theology of baptism in the form of a short historical sketch, showing the way in which Christians have talked about baptism at different periods of the Church's history, so that as a result of this survey the main themes of baptismal theology may stand out clearly.

In the first four chapters the teaching of the New Testament and of the Fathers will be considered. It is important to remember that in New Testament times and in the early centuries of the Christian era, the Church was dealing largely with adult converts, so that the Church's baptismal teaching and practice were geared to the needs of adults. The justification and meaning of infant baptism will be considered later, but in reading the earlier chapters it will be useful to bear in mind that we are concerned with adult baptism as the norm. The early period will be dealt with in more detail, since from the close of the patristic period the baptismal liturgies tended towards greater uniformity, and much of the greatest creative thinking in the Church had already been achieved.

Chapter 5 deals with the theology of baptism in the mediaeval period, up to and including the Council of Trent, and Chapter 6 deals with baptism in the modern world.

It is hoped that the picture of baptism which emerges from this survey will be a rich and varied one. In our thinking about baptism we in the West have sometimes tended perhaps to overstress the idea of baptism as a cleansing from original sin, whereas the biblical and patristic writers use a wide range of symbols and imagery to express the different aspects of the new life brought by baptism. Since all the topics of theology are inter-related, in talking about baptism we are often talking about salvation, and the way in which we think of salvation will shape our understanding of baptism. The early Fathers had a variety of ways of thinking about salvation, and they had a corresponding variety of ways of thinking about baptism.

Some of the traditional ways of thinking about baptism may have become so familiar to us that we find it hard to see through them as it were to the reality which these traditional symbols express. For the early Christians, baptism was a new and glorious event, marking the beginning of their new life in Christ. In studying the biblical and patristic understanding of baptism, may we recapture something of the joy and enthusiasm which this great sacrament inspired in the early Christians.

CHAPTER 1

BAPTISM IN THE NEW TESTAMENT

John's baptism

The theological foundation of Christian baptism lies for the New Testament writers in the death and resurrection of Christ. The word 'baptism' itself comes from a Greek verb meaning 'to dip'. The form which Christian baptism took was probably influenced by Jesus' baptism at the hands of John the Baptist. John's baptism in its turn may have been based on the Jewish custom of proselyte baptism. Male Gentile converts were received into the Jewish community by baptism and circumcision; women were received by baptism alone. The writings of the rabbis show that proselyte baptism was being practised towards the end of the first century A.D., but it is quite possible that it was already being employed at the time of our Lord, and even earlier. It is unlikely that the Jews would have adopted baptism after it had become established as the Christian rite of initiation.

John the Baptist may also have been influenced by the Qumran sect, about whom we learn in the Dead Sea scrolls, and who are probably to be identified with the Essenes described by the Jewish historian Josephus. The Qumran covenanters had frequent ritual ablutions, and practised baptism as the rite of reception into their community, but these baptisms were repeated. John's baptism resembles proselyte baptism in that both were once-for-all acts. If there are resemblances between John's baptism and proselyte baptism, there are also striking differences. In proselyte baptism, unlike John's, the neophyte baptized himself. Proselyte baptism was given only to Gentiles, whereas for John it is the Jewish people themselves who must undergo this rite as a sign

13

of repentance, if they are to become members of the true people of God, and able to face the coming day of wrath, which John saw as imminent. John the Baptist stands firmly in the prophetic tradition by his insistence that it is not racial descent from Abraham, but repentance and right living, that make the people acceptable to God.

Water is used in many religions as a symbol of cleansing and purification. The Jews practised frequent ritual washings, and these washings came to be seen as having a moral significance, expressing the worshipper's repentance and desire to be freed from sin (cf. Ps 51.7). The Jews looked forward to a future cleansing which would mean a complete purification from sin: 'I will sprinkle clean water upon you, and you shall be clean from all your uncleannesses, and from all your idols I will cleanse you' (Ezek 36.25; cf. Zech 13.1). The baptism of John was not the fulfilment of this eschatological hope, but pointed towards its fulfilment. John distinguishes between his own baptism, and that of the one who is to come. He contrasts his own baptism with a future baptism with the Holy Spirit (Mk 1.8); in Mt 3.11 and Lk 3.16, the coming baptism is to be with Holy Spirit and with fire. John summoned the people to repent so that they might be prepared for the coming of the Messiah, whose work would be one both of judgment (fire in the Old Testament is a symbol of judgment, cf. Mal 3.1f.), and of salvation. The gift of the spirit characterizes the age of salvation (cf. Joel 2.28). The real difference between John's baptism and Christian baptism is that only Christian baptism gives the Holy Spirit (cf. Acts 19.1f.).

If John's baptism was a baptism for the remission of sins, how was it that Jesus, the sinless one, submitted to it? This was felt to be a problem by the early Church. In the explanatory dialogue in Mt 3.14-15, Jesus says, 'Let it be so now; for thus it is fitting for us to fulfil all righteousness.' The thought behind this saying is probably similar to that in Is 53.11: 'By his knowledge shall the righteous one, my servant, make many to be accounted righteous, and he shall bear their iniquities'. It is fitting for Jesus to be baptized, for his baptism shows him as the servant of the Lord, identifying himself with his people, and taking their sins upon himself. The words spoken from heaven at Jesus' baptism (Mk 1.11 and parallels in Mt and Lk) are probably a composite quotation from Ps 2.7, a messianic psalm: 'You are my son, today I have begotten you', and Is 42.1: 'Behold my servant, whom I uphold, my chosen, in whom my soul delights.' It thus represents a fusion of the idea of the kingly Messiah with that of the servant of the Lord in Isaiah. The descent of the Spirit upon Jesus is the anointing of the Messiah at the beginning of his public ministry to enable him to carry out his messianic task (cf. Lk 4.18, quoting Is 61.1-2; Acts 4.27; Heb 1.9). The association of Spirit and sonship is a prominent theme in St Paul's theology (cf. Gal 6.4), and its source is probably to be traced back to the baptism of Jesus himself.

The real 'baptism' of Jesus is his death. In two sayings Jesus refers to his death as a baptism (Mk 10.38; Lk 12.50). Jesus asks, 'Are you able to drink the cup that I drink, or to be baptized with the baptism with which I am baptized?' (Mk 10.38). In the Old Testament, the cup was a symbol both of joy and blessing (Ps 23.5) and of retribution and suffering (Ps 75.8f.; Is 51.17; Jer 49.12). Here, the cup is a symbol of Jesus' redemptive suffering as Messiah, and undergoing baptism is a sym-

15

bolic reference to his approaching suffering and death.

Water in the Old Testament is an ambivalent symbol. It can represent life and blessing; cf. Ps 23.2, and Jer 2.13, where God is the 'fountain of living waters'. It can also recall the destructive waters of chaos, and sinking beneath the waters can be a symbol of great distress and anguish, as in Ps 69.1f.:

Save me, O God,

for the waters have come up to my neck,

...I have come into deep waters,

and the flood sweeps over me.

In the Apocalypse, the sea represents the waters of primeval chaos, and is the source of evil. The new creation is characterized by the fact that 'the sea was no more' (Apoc 21.1).

Both these aspects of water symbolism are present in the New Testament understanding of baptism. The water of baptism is water of judgment, like the Flood (1 Pet 3.20 f.), and a grave in which man's sinful past is buried (Rom 6.3-4). The thought of Christs's triumph over disorder and evil, symbolized by the waters of chaos, is probably present in St Paul's mind in Romans 6. Christians by their baptism are made sharers in Christ's death, and their immersion in the baptismal waters is a kind of burial. The water of baptism is also the source of new life, the means by which man is reborn. 'Truly, truly I say to you, unless one is born of water and the spirit, he cannot enter the Kingdom of God' (Jn 3.5).

There is no evidence in the Gospels that Jesus himself baptized during his earthly life, except Jn 3.22, but this statement is corrected in 4.2; it was not Jesus himself who baptized, but his disciples. Some of Jesus' disciples had been disciples of John the Baptist, and Jesus may have authorized the carrying on of this baptismal rite, as a sign of repentance, at the beginning of his ministry. Since Christians are baptized into the death and resurrection of Christ, the use of Christian baptism presupposes that Christ's work on earth is complete.

Baptism in the name of Jesus

The early Church, in practising baptism, did so on the authority of her risen Lord (Mt 28.19; cf. Mk 16.16). In Acts baptism is carried out 'in the name of Jesus' (Acts 2.38; 10.48) or 'in the name of Jesus Christ' (Acts 8.16; 19.5). Baptism in the name of Christ is also presupposed by 1 Cor 1.13,15. Being baptized in Christ's name means that the baptized person now belongs to Christ. Since our earliest New Testament sources speak of baptism in the name of Jesus, it may be that the developed Trinitarian formula of Mt 28.19 represents a reading back of the Church's later liturgical practice into the time of the resurrection appearances. J. H. Crehan S.J., in *Early Christian Baptism and the Creed,* thinks that the Matthean command authorized the disciples to use the Trinitarian formula in the act of baptizing, while the language of Acts refers to the part taken in the rite by the candidate, invoking the name of Christ or expressing faith in Christ. Even if the Trinitarian formula was not used in the earliest days of the Church, such a formula is implicit in passages like 1 Cor 6.11, 'But you were washed, you were sanctified, you were justified in the name of the Lord Jesus and in the spirit of our God'.

Timothy is exhorted to 'take hold of the eternal life to which you were called when you made the good confession in the presence of many witnesses' (1 Tim 6.12). This is probably a reference to Timothy's baptismal confession of faith, made in a public manner, and laying upon him a binding obligation.

Professor Cullmann, in his book *Baptism in the New Testament,* holds that we have a trace in Acts 8.36 f. of what is probably the oldest baptismal ritual, in which an enquiry was made whether any hindrance existed, that

17

is, whether the candidate for baptism had fulfilled all the conditions demanded. The Ethiopian eunuch asks, 'See, here is water! what is to prevent my being baptized?' (Acts 8.36). Cullmann points out that the same Greek verb, meaning 'prevent' or 'hinder', is found in the accounts of Jesus' blessing children (Mk 10.13-14 and parallels), 'Let the children come to me, do not hinder them,' and he thinks that this incident was used by the early Church to justify the practice of infant baptism. Acts 8.37 is omitted by the oldest and best New Testament manuscripts, but it contains a very early profession of faith, 'I believe that Jesus Christ is the Son of God'.

In this short account we have the essentials of the baptismal rite. The eunuch has been instructed by Philip, he makes a profession of faith and receives baptism by immersion, which was the normal practice in the early Church. Here, as throughout the New Testament, faith and baptism are intimately related. St Paul especially brings out the indissoluble connection between baptism and faith. The believer's personal relationship with God in Christ is brought about by faith (Gal 3.26); in Gal 3.27 this relationship is achieved in baptism. The New Testament writers do not consider the case of a man who has faith but is not baptized, or who comes to baptism without faith. For them, faith finds expression in undergoing the rite of baptism.

Probably the earliest baptismal confession of faith was 'Jesus is Lord' (1 Cor 12.3; Rom 10.9), in contrast with the 'many gods' and 'many lords' of paganism (1 Cor 8.6), in contrast too with Emperor-worship, with its claim, 'Caesar is Lord'. The power to confess that Jesus is Lord comes from the Holy Spirit (1 Cor 12.3). The following text probably refers to baptism: 'If you confess with your lips that Jesus is Lord and believe in your heart that God raised him from the dead, you will be saved' (Rom 10.9-10). Note the juxtaposition of faith and outward confession, both being essential.

When the Evangelists came to write down the miracles performed by Jesus, they did so in the light of their experience of the risen Lord working in his Church through the sacraments. The early Christian, in reading a passage such as Mk 10.51:

And Jesus said, 'What do you want me to do for you?' And the blind man said to him, 'Master, let me receive my sight': —

would think of his own baptism in which he too, like the blind man, was enlightened and set on the road to salvation. The blind man in Jn 9 is sent to wash in the pool of Siloam, which represents 'the one who has been sent', Jesus, the Messiah. Thus we can see the healing miracles of the gospels not merely as actions performed by Jesus long ago during his earthly life, but also as symbols or parables of what he does continuously through his Church.

The effects of baptism

In any consideration of baptism, as of the Christian life as a whole, there is a tension between what has been achieved in baptism, and the complete fulfilment which still remains in the future. In baptism we become sons of God (Rom 8.14-16; Gal 4.6 f.), sharers in Christ's sonship; and yet St Paul can speak of creation waiting 'with eager longing for the revealing of the sons of God' (Rom 8.19), and can go on to say, 'We ourselves, who have the first fruits of the spirit, groan inwardly as we wait for our adoption as sons, the redemption of our bodies' (Rom 8.23).

The gift of the Holy Spirit in baptism is bound up with the coming of the new age, and the divine gift of salvation. At Pentecost the Spirit was poured out upon the messianic community, and those who are baptized share in that spirit; they have 'tasted the heavenly gift, and have become partakers of the Holy Spirit, and have

19

tasted the goodness of the word of God, and the powers of the age to come' (Heb 6.4f.). Because they possess the Holy Spirit, Christians can be described as those 'upon whom the end of the ages has come' (1 Cor 10.11). The Jews expected the gift of the spirit in the messianic age. For the early Christians, the messianic age had already broken into the present, with the coming of Jesus. They were already living in the new age, although the consummation was still to come. The spirit given in baptism is the pledge or guarantee of our final inheritance (Eph 1.14; 2 Cor 1.22). The Greek word translated 'guarantee' by the RSV is a commercial term, used of a first consignment or sample of goods. (St Paul, as the first Christian theologian, had to create a new theological vocabulary.) The Holy Spirit is also described as the 'first fruits' of our final redemption (Rom 8.23). The believer is anointed with the Holy Spirit in baptism, as Jesus himself was anointed at his baptism for his messianic task. The function of the spirit in baptism is also spoken of as 'sealing': 'Do not grieve the Spirit of God, in whom you were sealed for the day of redemption' (Eph 4.30; cf. 1 Cor 1.22; 1 Jn 2.20). In the second century, 'the seal' was a common way of speaking of baptism. With the spirit given in baptism, there begins a gradual process of transformation into the likeness of the glorified Lord (2 Cor 3.17-18).

Baptism replaces circumcision as the means by which new members are incorporated into the people of God (Acts 2.41). In circumcision a piece of skin was removed, but in baptism it is the 'body of the flesh' (Col 2.11), the old sinful existence, that is laid aside.

Baptism in St Paul

St Paul sees baptism as the antitype or fulfilment of the Exodus (1 Cor 10). The Israelites all passed through the sea and were 'baptized into Moses', united with their leader. St Paul presupposes here that all Christians have passed through the waters of baptism and have been baptized 'into Christ', the new head and leader of the people of God. Christians inherit the privileges of the old Israel. They are a 'chosen race, a royal priesthood, a holy nation, God's own people' (1 Pet 2.9).

For St Paul, baptism places the believer 'in Christ' or 'in the body of Christ,' through the Spirit. Baptism is the basis of the unity of the Church, and the Spirit is the bond of unity. 'For by one Spirit we were all baptized into one body – Jews or Greeks, slaves or free – and all were made to drink of one spirit' (1 Cor 12.13). For those who are baptized, the distinctions of race or class which formerly existed among them are no longer of any real significance. 'There is neither Jew nor Greek, there is neither slave nor free, there is neither male nor female; for you are all one in Christ Jesus' (Gal 3.28). Belonging to Christ through baptism involves belonging to the Christian community, and becoming members of one another. Christ creates a new unity and a new solidarity among men. For St Paul, the solidarity of mankind as a social organism is expressed by the phrase 'in Adam'. This solidarity by nature is a solidarity in sin, since each new member of the human family is born into a world already disrupted by sin and selfishness. Reconciliation with God is achieved for us by the life, death and resurrection of Christ, and is offered to us as a free gift of grace, giving us the possibility of a new relationship with God. Our solidarity 'in Adam' exists by nature, but our solidarity with and in Christ has to be voluntarily accepted and made our own.

According to Gen 1.27, man was created in the image of God. But man, left to himself, cannot fulfil the destiny for which he was created. Christ through his incarnation is the new Adam, the new and perfect man, in whom alone God's purpose in creation has been fully

21

realized. Christ is the true and perfect image of God, the founder, head and representative of the new humanity re-created in the image of God (Col 3.10; Rom 8.24), and Christians, by becoming 'members of Christ' in baptism, and by striving with God's help to live their lives as Christians, are being transformed into the image of Christ (2 Cor 2.18).

Baptism brings the baptized person into relationship with the once-for-all saving act of God in Christ. Through faith and baptism, we share in what happened to Christ, and in what he achieved for us. Our identification with Christ takes place in baptism (Gal 3.27). Christians are united with Christ in his death; 'One has died for all, therefore all have died' (2 Cor 5.14). These two aspects are brought together in Romans 6; baptism is the point at which the saving death of Christ becomes effective for the Christian. In baptism we die and rise again with Christ. 'We have been united with him in a death like his' (Rom 6.5); the word translated 'united' means literally 'grown together'. The Christian in baptism becomes, in an almost organic way, a sharer or partaker in the death of Christ. The disciple dies in baptism, is crucified with Christ (Gal 2.19-20), and buried with him (Rom 6.14; Col 2.12), in order that he may share in the resurrection life of his Lord.

> We were buried therefore with him by baptism into death, so that as Christ was raised from the dead by the glory of the Father, we too might walk in newness of life (Rom 6.14).

The result of baptism is an abiding life in Christ. This new life in Christ, sacramentally bestowed, ought to show itself in a new way of living. Often in St Paul a dogmatic statement of what has been done in us and for us through baptism is followed by a moral imperative: 'If we live by the Spirit, let us also walk in the Spirit' (Gal 5.25). St Paul can say, 'For he who has died is freed from sin' (Rom 6.7), but although the Christian is no longer a slave to sin, he has nevertheless to carry on a lifelong struggle against it (Rom 6.12). 'Those who belong to Christ have crucified the flesh with its passions and desires' (Gal 5.24), but the crucifixion of the 'flesh', which here stands for man in his opposition to God, does not happen once for all in baptism. St Paul says in 2 Cor 4.11, 'For while we live we are always being given up to death for Jesus' sake, so that the life of Jesus may be manifested in our mortal flesh'. The Christian's life, in the time between the resurrection and the second coming, is therefore one of suffering, but this suffering is a prelude to future glory. 'I consider that the sufferings of this present time are not worth comparing with the glory that is to be revealed to us' (Rom 8.18).

In one sense, baptism is a once-for-all event, bringing about death to sin, and life to God; in another sense it is only the beginning of a process. What was achieved by the death and resurrection of Christ, and appropriated in baptism, has to be made effective in the life of the believer. The relationship with God which baptism opens up to us has to be accepted and lived out in our daily lives. The consequence of baptism is not only that we live in Christ, but that he is our life, and that we shall share in the final manifestation of his glory (Col 3.4). Life in Christ and life in the Spirit are terms used interchangeably by St Paul. What is brought about in baptism is nothing less than a new creation: 'Therefore if any one is in Christ, he is a new creation' (2 Cor 5.17), although, here again, there is a tension between what we already possess by faith, and what we hope for.

Images used of baptism

The significance of baptism in the New Testament is brought out by the use of various metaphors. A constant theme is that of baptism as a means of cleansing and purification. Baptism is for the forgiveness of sins (Acts 22.16; 1 Cor 6.11; 2 Pet 1.9; Heb 10.3). But this cleansing is not merely negative, confined to the washing away of sin; the cleansing brought about by baptism reaches the innermost being, and it also imparts sanctification:

> Baptism, which corresponds to this (the Flood) now saves you, not as a removal of dirt from the body, but as an appeal to God for a clear conscience through the resurrection of Jesus Christ (1 Pet. 3.20).

There is probably a reference to baptism in Heb 10.22: 'with our bodies sprinkled clean from an evil conscience, and our bodies washed with pure water'. Christian baptism is an effective symbol, bringing about that inner cleansing which it outwardly represents. The cleansing power of baptism derives from the sacrificial death of Jesus (1 Jn 1.7; Apoc 7.14). The blood and water flowing from the pierced side of Christ on the cross (Jn 19.34) suggest the two sacraments of baptism and the Eucharist, through which the benefits of the Lord's death are communicated to the faithful. Baptism can be thought of as applied not only to the individual but also the Church; Christ gave himself up for the Church, 'that he might sanctify her, having cleansed her with the washing of water by the word' (Eph 5.26).

Baptism is also described in the New Testament, in the Johannine writings and 1 Peter, as a new birth. 'You have been born anew, not of perishable seed but of imperishable, through the living and abiding word of God' (1 Pet 1.23). St Paul does not use the metaphor of rebirth, perhaps because it was used in the mystery-religions, and would therefore be liable to be misunderstood by his Gentile readers. He speaks instead of our adoption as sons, and of the new creation. Sometimes the new birth of baptism is seen as taking place through the spirit (Jn 3.5), or baptism can be seen simply as a being begotten by God (1 Jn 5.18). The First Epistle of Peter speaks of rebirth as taking place through the resurrection; 'By his great mercy, we have been born anew to a living hope through the resurrection of Jesus Christ from the dead' (1 Pet 1.3).

Baptism is also 'the washing of regeneration and renewal in the Holy Spirit' (Tit 3.5). The word translated 'regeneration' occurs only twice in the New Testament. In Mt 19.28 it refers to the new creation at the end of time, whereas in Titus it refers to the renewal of the redeemed individual in the present time.

The change involved in becoming a Christian is also described in the New Testament as a transition from darkness to light. Christians are called upon to declare 'the wonderful deeds of him who called you out of darkness into his marvellous light' (1 Pet 2.9; cf. Jn 8.12; 1 Jn 1.6-7; 2 Cor 4.4-6).

'To be enlightened' (Heb 6.4 and 10.32) is a synonym for 'to be baptized'.

St Paul speaks of this change as a 'putting off' of the 'body of flesh' (Col 2.11), or of the old nature, or the death of our old self (Rom 6.6), which was crucified and buried with Christ, and the 'putting on' of Christ (Gal 3.27), or of the new nature (Col 3.10). Through baptism believers attain so close a union with Christ that they are wholly clothed with him.

From this survey we can collect a number of Biblical images used to describe what happens in baptism – washing or cleansing from sin, death and resurrection, rebirth, new creation, adoption as God's sons, becoming temples of the Spirit and members of Christ. These and the other great Biblical images remain normative for our understanding of baptism, and they occur again and again in the writings of the Fathers. Underlying all these images are the two basic aspects of Christian baptism; baptism brings about a relationship to Christ, and a relationship to the Church. These are not of course two separate aspects; baptism brings about a relationship to Christ in and through his Church.

CHAPTER 2

BAPTISM IN THE SECOND CENTURY

There is no complete treatise on baptism until the end of the second century, with Tertullian's *On Baptism*. Otherwise we have only scattered references to baptism in the writings of the Church Fathers of this period, who are known as the Apostolic Fathers.

Ignatius of Antioch

St Ignatius, bishop of Antioch, was martyred at Rome some time during the reign of Trajan (98-117 A.D.). On his journey from Antioch to Rome, where he was to die, Ignatius wrote letters to seven churches in Asia Minor. In his letter to the Ephesians he says of Jesus, 'He was born and baptized that by his passion he might hallow water' (*Ephes*. 18). The sacrament of baptism is so important for Ignatius that he can see the hallowing of the baptismal water as the purpose of Christ's death.

In his letter to Polycarp, bishop of Smyrna, Ignatius uses the imagery of military service to describe the Christian life:

Let none of you be found to be a deserter, let your baptism remain as your arms; your faith as your helmet; your love as your spear; your endurance as your armour (*Polyc*. 6.2).

The Didachē

The earliest description of baptism that we have outside the New Testament is to be found in the *Didachē* or 'Teaching of the Twelve Apostles'. This document was only known to us from other early Christian writings until it was rediscovered in 1873. The date of the *Didachē* is uncertain, but it comes from a Jewish-Christian milieu, probably at the beginning of the second century. The *Didachē*, true to its title, begins with moral instruction, speaking of the two ways of life and of death, and describing the way in which a Christian ought to behave. The early Christians, like the Jews, had a probationary period for would-be converts (the catechumenate), during which candidates for baptism were instructed and their lives examined to see if they were worthy to be received. By the third century, the catechumenate had become a well organized institution.

The Didachē goes on to describe the way in which baptism is to be administered:

> Now concerning baptism; this is how to baptize. Give public instruction on all these matters [probably the questions of conduct and ethics dealt with in sections 1-6], and then baptize in running water, in the name of the Father and of the Son and of the Holy Spirit. If you do not have running water, baptize in some other. If you cannot baptize in cold water, then do so in warm. If you have neither, then pour water on the head three times in the name of the Father and of the Son and of the Holy Spirit. Before the baptism, moreover, the one who baptizes and the one who is being baptized must fast, and any others who can. And you must tell the one who is being baptized to fast for one or two days beforehand (*Did.* 7).

The *Didachē* recognizes both baptism by immersion and baptism by infusion (pouring). Baptism by total immersion was the normal practice in the early Church, and baptism by total or partial immersion is still practised by the Eastern Churches. The *Didachē* regards baptism in flowing water as normal; this method of baptism was probably in imitation of Jesus' baptism in the Jordan.

The Epistle of Barnabas

This is another Jewish-Christian document, to be dated probably in the early second century. It contains a chapter 'Concerning the water and the cross'. Here the writer expounds various Old Testament texts which throw light for him on baptism. Commenting on Ps 1.3, 'He [the just man] is like a tree, planted by streams of water,' the writer says, 'Blessed are those who set their hope on the cross, and go down into the water' (*Barn.* 11). Again, commenting on Ezek 47.12, the writer speaks of the descent into the baptismal waters, with their sanctifying power.

> 'And there was a river flowing from the right hand, and beautiful trees rose up from it, and whoever eats of them will live forever' (Ezek 47.12). He says this, because we go down into the water laden with sins and filth, and rise up from it bearing fruit in our hearts, resting our fear and hope on Jesus in the Spirit. 'And whoever eats of them shall live for ever'; he means this: whoever, he says, hears these things spoken and believes, will live for ever (*Barn.* 11).

Hermas

From the same Jewish-Christian milieu, about the middle of the second century, comes the strange work known as the *Shepherd of Hermas*. 'Hermas' has a series of visions which are interpreted for him by the shepherd, or angel of repentance. The writer has a strong sense of the ethical implications of baptism, leading him to rigorism; there can be no forgiveness for serious post-baptismal sin. Hermas is told by the shepherd that there is indeed no other repentance except that of baptism. 'He who has received remission of sins ought no longer to

29

, but to dwell in purity' (*Mandate* 4.3). The rigorism Hermas is tempered by the statement that the Christians of his generation are being given one opportunity of a second repentance.

Hermas sees baptism as the foundation of the Christian life. He sees in a vision six young men building a tower with stones. He is told that the tower represents the Church, and asks why the tower is being built on water. The woman who represents the Church tells him, 'It is because your life is saved and will be saved by water' (*Vis.* 3.3).

Hermas refers to the epiclesis, or invocation of the divine name, over the baptismal water. He speaks of 'the name of the Son of God' only; in later liturgies the Trinity is invoked as the candidate goes down into the water. The Shepherd tells Hermas, 'If therefore you bear the name, and do not bear his power, you will bear his name to no avail' (*Simil.* 9.12f.). So essential is baptism for salvation, according to Hermas, that the righteous of the old dispensation had to be baptized before they could enter heaven.

The Odes of Solomon

The *Odes of Solomon* also come from a Jewish-Christian milieu, probably about the middle of the second century. These odes may have been intended for liturgical use; they all end with 'Alleluia!' and it has been suggested that they were hymns for the catechumens or newly-baptized. In these hymns there are references to baptismal customs characteristic of Syria; the newly-baptized were crowned with garlands, and, as in other rites, given milk and honey to symbolize their entry through baptism into the new Promised Land. The *Odes of Solomon* celebrate with exultant joy the new life brought by baptism:

I was established upon the rock of tru
had set me up; and speaking water touch.
from the fountain of the Lord plenteous
drank and was inebriated with the livin,
which does not die (11.3f.).

Other hymns are invitations to baptism:

Fill ye waters for yourselves from the living foun.
tain of the Lord, for it is open to you; and come all
ye thirsty, and take the draught, and rest by the
fountain of the Lord (30).

In the baptismal ritual, after the renunciation of the devil,
the catechumens, with their hands outstretched in the
form of a cross, faced east and professed their allegiance
to Christ, 'I stretched out my hand and sanctified my
Lord; for the extension of my hands is his sign' (27.1).

In Syriac, the word for 'spirit' is feminine (as in other
Semitic languages), and the Holy Spirit is regarded as a
mother.

As the wings of doves over their nestlings, and the
mouth of nestlings toward their mouths, so also are
the wings of the Spirit over my heart; my heart is
delighted and exults, like the babe who exults in the
womb of his mother (28.1f.).

God the Father is also depicted as a mother, from whose
breasts the faithful are suckled:

Love me with affection, ye who love; for I do not
turn away my face from them that are mine; for I
know them, and before they came into being I took
knowledge of them, and on their faces I set my
seal; I fashioned their members; my own breasts I
prepared for them, that they might drink my holy
spirit and live thereby (7.14f.).

Baptism, in Jewish-Christian rites especially, is often
spoken of as a seal. This 'seal' in early Christian baptism was probably a mark made on the forehead. Ezek-

31

mark placed on the foreheads of the righ-
ourn over the sins of their people (Ezek
gn was the Hebrew letter *tau* which in its
n was written + or X. Similarly in the Apoca-
elect are marked with the seal of God on their
s, as a sign that they belong to him. Thus, the
n Jewish Christianity was probably the *tau*
ed on the forehead as a sign that the baptized per-
belonged to God. In a non-Jewish environment, this
rk was interpreted not as *tau* but as the sign of the
oss or as a reference to Christ.

Justin Martyr

The earliest description of the baptismal liturgy in the
West comes from Justin, who belongs to the second century group of Fathers known as the Apologists. The aim
of the Apologists was to present the Christian faith in
terms intelligible and acceptable to the educated pagan
of the time, and by showing the high moral standards
and beneficial effects of Christianity, the Apologists
hoped to win at least tolerance for their faith, if not
complete acceptance of it. Because they were writing for
pagans, the Apologists were normally guarded in their
language; they did not want to reveal all the doctrines of
Christianity to the uninitiated who might misunderstand
them. Justin, however, in his *First Apology*, written
about 155 A.D. and addressed to the Emperor Antoni-
nus Pius, gives a description of the preparation for baptism, and of the rite itself. Baptism is preceded by a
period of instruction; the immediate preparation is
prayer and fasting.

Then they [the candidates] are brought by us where
there is water, and are reborn by the same manner
of rebirth by which we ourselves were reborn; for
they are then washed in the water in the name of

God the Father and Master of all, and of ou
viour Jesus Christ, and of the Holy Spirit... So
we should not remain children of necessity and
norance, but be sons of free choice and knowledg
and obtain forgiveness of the sins we have already
committed, there is named at the water, over the
one who has chosen to be born again and has re-
pented of his sins, the name of God the Father and
Master of all... This washing is called enlightenment, since those who learn these things are inwardly enlightened. The enlightened one is also
washed in the name of Jesus Christ, who was crucified under Pontius Pilate, and in the name of the
Holy Spirit, who through the prophets foretold
everything about Jesus (*Apol.* 1.61).

Justin gives a description of the preparation for baptism,
and of the effects of baptism; baptism brings about rebirth, remission of sins and enlightenment. The candidate for baptism must believe in the truth of Christian
teaching and practice, and must be prepared to live accordingly; he must have faith and repent of his sins.

In all the early rites the sacrament of Christian initiation formed a whole; there was no separation between
'baptism' and 'confirmation'. It was only later in the
West that the two rites became separated, and confirmation was associated with a special outpouring of the spirit.

In all these texts, the idea emerges of baptism as a
water-bath or washing which, through the invocation of
the divine names, brings about remission of sins, and
leads to rebirth, entry into God's kingdom, and salvation. The way in which the effects of baptism are described depends on the thought-world of the different
writers; for Justin, the effects of baptism include knowledge and illumination. All the writers of this period
agree in stressing both the moral preparation for baptism
and its moral consequences. The transformation brought

33

y baptism must show itself in the life of the bap-

CHAPTER 3

BAPTISM IN THE EASTERN CHURCH

Since it is impossible in a book of this size to do more than give a very selective account of patristic writings on baptism, a few patristic texts have been chosen to illustrate the main tendencies of baptismal theology in East and West. Among the Fathers who wrote complete treatises on baptism are, in the East, St Cyril of Jerusalem, St John Chrysostom and Theodore of Mopsuestia, and in the West, Tertullian, St Ambrose and St Augustine.

Clement of Alexandria

Clement of Alexandria (d.215) was a disciple of Pantaenus, and succeeded him as the principal teacher of the Christian faith at Alexandria, where there was in effect a Christian university. Clement, as a Christian educator, was concerned with moral teaching. He also stressed, and perhaps overstressed, the role of knowledge in the Christian life.

Clement, writing in the last decade of the second century, speaks of baptism as 'enlightenment', involving rebirth, cleansing and the remission of sins:

> When we are baptized, we are enlightened; being enlightened, we are made sons; being made sons, we are made perfect; and being made perfect, we are made divine... This ceremony is often called 'free gift', since by it the punishments due to our sins are remitted; 'enlightenment', since by it we behold the holy light of salvation, that is, through it we are enabled to see the divine; we call it 'perfection', needing nothing more; for what more does he need who has the knowledge of God? (*Paed.* 1.6.26).

In this passage we find several ideas characteristic of the Greek Fathers. There is the idea that through baptism, we become divine, that is, partakers of the divine nature. The Greek Fathers often speak of salvation as divinisation. They also stress the importance of knowledge of God. Faith for Clement is the perfection of knowledge:

> Those who are baptized are cleansed of the sins which overcloud their divine spirit like a mist, and they acquire a spiritual sight which is free and unhindered and clear, by which alone we are able to behold divinity, with the help of the Holy Spirit, who flows in upon us from heaven (*ibid*. 1.6.28).

The key words in Clement's discussion of baptism are 'knowledge', 'enlightenment', 'faith'. These themes recur in the writings of Clement's successor and disciple, the great Church Father Origen.

Origen (d. 254)

Origen, the son of a martyr, Leonides, was, while still a very young man, appointed by his bishop head of the catechetical school at Alexandria. Later, on being expelled from Alexandria, Origen founded a new school in Caesarea. He was a great theologian, philosopher, and mystic, and a prolific writer on biblical exegesis, apologetics and theology. Like all the Fathers, Origen uses Biblical imagery and Old Testament symbols to describe baptism. Baptism is a new Exodus, and the means by which the catechumen is set free from the devil. For Origen, there are three kinds of baptism: the baptism of the Old Testament, at the Exodus, in the cloud and the sea, which is, like John's baptism, a symbol of Christian baptism; secondly, Christian baptism, which gives the spirit, and is both the reality signified by Old Testament baptism, and a symbol of the baptism to come; and finally the eschatological baptism with the spirit and with fire, which will be conferred upon all Christians before they enter into glory.

The practice of infant baptism in the East is attested by Origen. He argues from the fact that the Church's baptism is given for the remission of sins to the conclusion that if infants are baptized, it is because there is sin in them which must be remitted (*In Lev. Hom.* 8.3). In support of his position Origen quotes Ps 51.3: 'Behold I was brought forth in iniquity, and in sin did my mother conceive me.'

Origen stresses the necessity of moral preparation for baptism, although he regards the sacrament as producing its effect by its own inherent power.

Baptismal liturgies

The baptismal liturgies presupposed by St Cyril, St John Chrysostom and Theodore of Mopsuestia are similar in outline. Theodore of Mopsuestia, in his *Commentary on the Sacrament of Baptism*, describes how the candidates were brought to the registrar of baptisms by their godparents, who had to vouch for their suitability. The registrar questioned the candidates about their manner of life.

Exorcisms played an important part in the catechumens' preparation for baptism. During the exorcisms the candidates took off their outer garments and stood on sackcloth, bare-footed, with hands outstretched to heaven. This posture was a symbol of their servitude to the devil.

All three writers speak of the renunciation of Satan, which was made at the beginning of the ceremony of baptism, while the candidates faced West. Then they turned to the East and made a profession of faith. Chrysostom and Theodore have at this point the anointing of the candidate by the bishop, with the formula, 'N. is anointed in the name of the Father and of the Son and of the Holy Spirit'. This passive formula is still used by the Eastern Churches, in contrast with the indicative formula of the Roman Church, 'I baptize thee...' The passive formula is intended to emphasize that the priest is only an instrument, and that baptism is the work of God. After baptism, Cyril and Theodore speak of the white garments, a sign of joy and blessing, with which the candidates were clothed. After this, Theodore alone mentions a signing of the candidates on the forehead by the bishop. The candidates then proceeded to the Church, where they received their first communion. These ceremonies are broadly the same as those we shall be considering in the West.

St Cyril of Jerusalem

St Cyril was a monk, and became bishop of Jerusalem about the year 348 A.D. It was perhaps in the Lent of that year that his lectures on the Christian Sacraments were delivered to the catechumens who were preparing for baptism. The last five lectures, known as the mystagogical catecheses (from the Greek *mustēs,* 'initiate'), were given during Easter week to the newly baptized. In his teaching on the sacraments, St Cyril is handing on the tradition of the Church as he had received it. Like all the Fathers, St Cyril holds that baptism is essential for salvation; it can however be replaced by 'baptism of blood', or martyrdom. Like Tertullian and Cyprian, Cyril believes that heretic baptism is invalid. St. Cyril warns the catechumens not to speak of the 'mystery' which is being delivered to them, the hope of the life to come. The catechumens who have been enrolled have become 'the sons and daughters of one Mother', the Church (*Protocat.* 13). St Cyril celebrates the greatness of the baptism which is offered to them:

38

It is a ransom for captives; the remission of offences; the death of sin; the regeneration of the soul; the garment of light; holy indissoluble seal; the chariot to heaven; the luxury of Paradise; the gift of adoption (*Protocat.* 16).

The water of baptism 'was at once your grave and your mother' (*Cat. Myst.* 2.4). In this rite in which we imitate in a figure the death, burial and resurrection of Christ, salvation is brought about not in a figure but in reality.

The post-baptismal anointing with chrism on forehead, ears, nostrils and breast brings the gift of the Holy Spirit. St Cyril develops the significance of each anointing, concluding:

For as Christ after his baptism and the descent of the Holy Spirit went out and overcame the enemy, so likewise, after baptism and the mystical chrism, having put on the armour of the Holy Spirit, you must stand against the power of the enemy, and overcome it, saying, 'I can do all things in him who strengthens me' (*Cat. Myst.* 3.4).

St John Chrysostom

St John Chrysostom was born c.344. He became Bishop of Constantinople. His outstanding gifts as a preacher earned him the name of Chrysostom, 'golden-mouthed'. Chrysostom's interest lay not in philosophy or speculation, but in the spiritual life and the inculcation of true morals.

Chrysostom delivered a number of baptismal homilies at Antioch. He invites the catechumens to the spiritual marriage, addressing each of them as a 'bride who is about to be brought into her holy bridal chamber' (Wenger, 1.3). The baptismal robe is a symbol of Christ, whom the neophyte has put on. The 'bridal feast' of baptism is prolonged for seven days (as it was during the

Easter octave in the Roman Church). Chrysostom points out that the feast is not prolonged for seven days only: 'If you are willing to live soberly and to be watchful, these feasts are prolonged for you throughout all time, provided that you keep your bridal robe inviolate and radiant' (Wenger, 6.24).

Chrysostom lays special stress on the presence of Christ in the baptized. The purpose of the exorcisms is to prepare a dwelling worthy of this presence.

Baptism is a preparation for the Christian life, which is a warfare against the devil. The catechumens are soldiers of Christ, 'those who have enlisted in this special spiritual army' (Wenger 1.20). After renouncing Satan, the candidate for baptism says, 'And I attach myself to thee, O Christ.' Then he is anointed, as a soldier chosen for the spiritual arena (Wenger 2.21-22). From this time onwards there is strife between the devil and the baptized.

Chrysostom is fond of using athletic metaphors to describe the Christian life. The thirty days of instruction for baptism are compared to the bodily exercises of a wrestling-school. The catechumens are to learn how to gain the advantage over the devil; after baptism the contest will begin in earnest.

Baptism brings about not only remission of sins, but also regeneration. In baptism we are re-created and fashioned anew. Chrysostom uses the image of a golden statue which has become filthy over the years, but which is melted down and becomes clear and shining. So God takes our nature rusted with sin, and smelts it again. Water replaces the smelting furnace, and the Holy Spirit the flames. The old man is broken in pieces, and the new man is produced (PG 49.227).

Another image Chrysostom uses is that of a painting. Before the true colour of the spirit can be put on, bad habits must be erased, lest the candidate should return to them after baptism;

The bath removes the sins, but you must correct the habit, so that after the paint is put on and the royal image shines forth, you may never afterwards wipe it out or produce wounds or scars on the beauty which God has given you (PG 49.235).

The greatness of the gifts received in baptism makes it necessary for the neophytes to show forth the fruits of baptism in their lives. Dignitaries who wear the imperial image on their clothing have to act in a fitting way. Christians have Christ not on their clothing but dwelling in their souls, with the Father and the Spirit. Christians must therefore show by their lives that they too are wearing the imperial image (Wenger 4.17).

Chrysostom's homilies contain frequent moral exhortation. He is concerned primarily, as other Eastern Fathers were, with baptism in its relation to the spiritual life. Perhaps the chief glory of baptism for St John Chrysostom is that it brings about the indwelling of Christ in the one baptized.

Theodore of Mopsuestia

Theodore, born c. 350 at Antioch, was bishop of Mopsuestia in Cilicia. He opposed the Monophysite heresy of Apollinaris but has himself been regarded, in many ways unjustly, as the father of Nestorianism. Theodore's thought was biblical and pictorial rather than metaphysical, but within the context of his own framework of thought Theodore was essentially orthodox.

Theodore sees the sacraments in their relation to the Christian life. His conception of the Christian life is orientated towards heaven, and is expressed in terms of the 'two ages', present and future. The second age began with the redeeming work of Christ, which marks the beginning of the restoration of both man and creation to the state which obtained before the Fall. The life of the

Church and of Christians, including therefore the sacraments, provide a model or pattern of life in heaven, just as the symbols of the Old Testament provide a pattern for the Church.

Theodore thinks of the sacraments as orientated towards the future, giving the Christian a foretaste of those realities which he will only experience fully in the world to come. Baptism is a symbol of the new birth we are expecting, the true second birth which we will only undergo at the resurrection. Theodore's conception of baptism, like Origen's, is eschatological. But baptism is not simply the symbol of a reality which is still to come; through baptism we already participate in a salvation the full enjoyment of which lies in the future:

> The power of the holy baptism consists in this; it implants in you the hope of the future benefits, enables you to participate in the good things which we expect, and by means of the symbols and signs of the future good things, it informs you with the gift of the Holy Spirit (*Commentary on the Sacrament of Baptism,* 4).

Every sacrament, says Theodore, consists in the 'representation of unseen and unspeakable things through signs and symbols' (*ibid.* 2). Baptism is a participation in the death and resurrection of Christ, and the means of becoming a citizen of the heavenly kingdom. Through baptism the image of God, which man had lost through sin, is restored. In baptism we are reborn and become symbolically immortal. The water of baptism is a tomb and also a womb in which the new man is born of Christ. The baptismal water is also like a furnace in which the catechumen is renewed and refashioned, having cast away his old mortality and put on 'an immortal and incorruptible nature'.

The benefits of baptism Theodore lists as:
second birth, renewal, immortality, deliverance from impassibility, immutability, deliverance from death

42

and servitude and all evils, happiness of freedom, and participation in the ineffable good things we are expecting (*ibid*. 4).

These blessings spring from the nature of baptism as the Eastern Fathers conceived it; salvation for them was primarily a sharing in the divine nature, and therefore sharing, in so far as it is possible for man, in the attributes of the divine nature, such as immortality and impassibility. The Fathers whose writings we have glanced at continue also to use biblical imagery to describe baptism. Perhaps the most characteristic emphasis of Eastern baptismal theology is the parallel which the Eastern Fathers, from Origen onwards, draw between the theology of the sacraments and the theology of the spiritual life.

St Ephraim

The Eastern Fathers celebrate the greatness of the 'mystery' of baptism. The joy of the redeemed is expressed in the hymns of St Ephraim, a fourth-century Syrian Father, who was born at Nisibis and finally settled at Edessa. His hymns were probably composed for the feast of the Epiphany, and they express the rejoicing of the newly-baptized: 'The sheep of Christ leaped for joy, to receive the seal of life, that ensign of kings which has ever put sin to flight' (3.24). In baptism, the evil one is put to flight 'in the chrism of Christ, and in the armour which is from the water' (5.11). The baptized are the sheep of Christ, 'lambs new-born and spiritual', stamped with his seal, the Cross. The newly-baptized are given lamps, which symbolize the enlightenment which they, like the blind man at the pool of Siloam, have received: 'from the water ye have been clad in light' (7.22). The baptized are clothed in glory: 'For the sheep that are white of heart, gaze on the glory that is in the water; in your souls reflect ye it' (9.6).

Crowns are given to the newly-baptized. They have come up from the water 'in the likeness of angels' and 'in the armour of the Holy Ghost' (13.1-2). Baptism brings with it pardon for sin, sanctification, the gift of the Holy Spirit, and glory. The hymn of the baptized, Hymn 13, is a continuous cry of praise and thanksgiving for the blessings of baptism: 'Glory to them, that are robed, glory to Adam's house – in the birth that is from the water, let them rejoice and be blessed!' (13.21).

It can be said in conclusion that the early Fathers, especially in the East, were concerned with celebrating the greatness of baptism and the blessings that it brings, rather than with a detailed theological analysis of the sacrament.

CHAPTER 4

BAPTISM IN THE WESTERN CHURCH

Tertullian

Tertullian, the great African Church Father, who eventually fell into the rigorist Montanist heresy, wrote his treatise *On Baptism* at the end of the second century. He presents us with an already developed theology of baptism. The details of the baptismal rite which we gather from Tertullian are similar to those described in the slightly later liturgy of Hippolytus. In Tertullian's case we have to reconstruct the ritual from scattered references in his works. Tertullian's rite included a renunciation of the devil and of the world, a prayer to sanctify the water, and baptism with triple immersion, followed by an anointing with blessed oil.

In early Christian art, the fish was used as a symbol of Christ, partly because the letters of the Greek word for fish (*ichthus*) were the initial letters of 'Jesus Christ, Son of God, Saviour'. Tertullian says, 'But we little fish, as Jesus Christ is our great fish, are born in the water, and only while we remain in the water are we safe' (*De Bapt.* 1).

The baptismal water is sanctified by the power of the Holy Spirit. Tertullian sees the power of the waters at Bethzatha (Jn 5.2f.) to bring about bodily healing, when stirred by an angel, as prophetic of the spiritual healing brought about by baptism. By baptism there is restored to man the image of God in which he was created. Tertullian speaks of the Old Testament types of baptism, primarily the Exodus. Commenting on the incident in Exod 15.23-25, where bitter water is restored to sweetness by the tree that Moses threw in, Tertullian says:

That tree was Christ, who from within himself

45

heals the springs of that nature which was formerly poisoned and bitter, changing them into the most healthgiving water of baptism (*ibid*. 9).

Tertullian speaks of the rule that, without baptism, no one can attain salvation. The apostles were saved through faith in Christ, although they were not baptized, but Tertullian combats the view of those who say that, since salvation is by faith, baptism is unnecessary. This was so before the resurrection, but now the 'seal of baptism' is necessary for all.

Tertullian emphasizes that baptism is one and unrepeatable. He denies that heretics have true baptism. A great controversy was to arise in the third and fourth centuries about the question of the validity of heretic baptism.

Tertullian believes that sin should not be committed after baptism, since the forgiveness of sins granted in baptism is once-for-all. 'We enter then once into the bath, once are our sins washed away, because they ought not to be repeated' (*ibid*. 15). This attitude was not peculiar to Tertullian. For most early Christians, whose conversion had involved an intense personal crisis and a complete break with their former way of life, baptism was seen as the gift of a new life, in which sin could have no place. They were unable to reconcile themselves to the idea of post-baptismal sin. The only 'second washing' which Tertullian recognizes is the 'Washing of blood' (martyrdom).

For Tertullian, the supreme right of baptizing belongs to the bishop. Presbyters and deacons can also baptize, with a commission from the bishop. Somewhat reluctantly, Tertullian admits the right of the laity (though not of women) to confer baptism in case of emergency.

Baptism is not to be given lightly, and it may often be profitable to defer it. Tertullian's awareness of the obligations imposed by baptism leads him to say, 'Any one who understands the importance of baptism will have more fear of obtaining it than of postponing it' (*ibid*. 18). In the fourth century there was a tendency to postpone baptism for this reason, sometimes until the deathbed. Tertullian sees delay as being especially profitable in the case of children. They should come to be baptized when they have learned to know Christ. 'Why should the age of innocence hasten to the remission of sins?' (*ibid*. 18).

The Passover (Easter) is the most solemn day for baptism, and Pentecost the next, but, he says, 'Every day is a Lord's day; any hour, any season is suitable for baptism; if there is a difference of solemnity, there is no difference in the grace' (*ibid*. 19). Those who are about to be baptized ought to pray frequently, with fasting and confession of all their former sins. In his treatise *Adversus Praxean*, Tertullian links the threefold immersion with the Trinity: 'for not once only but three times are we baptized into each of the three persons at each of the names' (*Adv. Prax.* 26).

This treatise of Tertullian brings up two points which were to be dealt with more fully by later writers; the validity of baptism given outside the Church, and the question of the rationale of infant baptism.

Hippolytus

The *Apostolic Tradition* of Hippolytus is a Roman liturgical document, coming from the beginning of the third century. Hippolytus (c. 170-235 A.D.) was a Roman priest who became anti-Pope in opposition to Pope Zephyrinus, but died a martyr's death in 235. The *Apostolic Tradition* seems to provide evidence that infant baptism was being practised by this time. It is possible of course that the practice of infant baptism goes back for a long time before this.

Admission to the catechumenate was strictly supervised. Candidates were brought normally by Christian friends, who had to vouch for them. The candidates were examined by 'teachers' as to their motives in coming forward for admission to the Church, and their manner of life. The catechumenate normally lasted three years, but this period of preparation could be shortened if the candidate showed good will and perseverance. Each period of instruction ended with a prayer, after which the teacher, whether he was an ecclesiastic or a layman, laid his hands on the candidates and dismissed them. Catechumens were told not to be anxious if they were arrested for their faith before they had been baptized, for if a catechumen is put to death before receiving baptism, 'he will be justified, having received baptism in his own blood' (19.2). 'Baptism of blood' could thus replace the sacrament of baptism.

Those who were chosen to receive baptism (the *electi*), were again examined as to their manner of life. They then received daily exorcism and laying on of hands, and when the day for baptism drew near, each one was exorcised by the bishop himself. Those who were to be baptized on the Sunday were instructed to wash and cleanse themselves on the Thursday, and to fast on Friday and Saturday. A final reunion of the *electi* was held on Saturday evening, presided over by the bishop. They prayed, kneeling, then the bishop laid his hands on them and exorcised them. Next the bishop breathed on their faces (this ceremony was known as exsufflation and was an expression of contempt for the devil). He then anointed ('sealed') their foreheads, ears and noses, and raised them up. The whole night was spent in vigil, with reading of the scriptures and instruction.

At cockcrow, there was a prayer over the water. The candidates undressed. Children were baptized first, then men, then women, who had to loose their hair and lay aside their ornaments. The bishop gave thanks over some oil, which was known as the 'oil of thanksgiving';

more oil was blessed as the 'oil of exorcism'. Each candidate, supervised by the priest, said, 'I renounce thee, Satan, and all thy service and all thy works.' He was then anointed with the oil of exorcism. The candidate stood naked in the water, while the bishop or priest who baptized him laid his hand on the candidate's head and immersed him three times with a triple interrogation:

Do you believe in God the Father Almighty?
Do you believe in Jesus Christ, the Son of God, who was born of the Holy Spirit and the Virgin Mary?
Do you believe in the Holy Spirit in the Holy Church, and the resurrection of the flesh?

To each question the candidate replied, 'I believe'. When he came out of the water, he was anointed with the oil of thanksgiving, with the words, 'I anoint thee with holy oil in the name of Jesus Christ'. Afterwards the bishop laid his hands on the candidates and anointed their foreheads with blessed oil. The sacrament of 'confirmation' had not yet been separated from baptism.

St Ambrose

St Ambrose gave up an administrative career to become bishop of Milan in 374 A.D. He played an important part not only as a pastor but as a Christian statesman, and he was noted as a fine orator. St Ambrose's treatise *On the Sacraments* c. 390 A.D. consists of six short addresses to the neophytes, delivered from the Tuesday of Easter week to Low Sunday. These addresses were published in condensed form as *On the Mysteries*. St Ambrose speaks of baptism as the fulfilment of the Exodus. The Hebrews, who had passed through the Red Sea, died in the desert.

But the man who passes through this font, that is from the earthly to the heavenly – the passage from sin to life, from fault to grace, from defilement to sanctification – the man who passes through this font does not die but rises (*De Sacram.* 1.4.12).

The water itself does not have power to cleanse; the cure is effected by the operation of the Holy Spirit. Commenting on Rom 6.3, St Ambrose speaks of baptism into the death of Christ:

> For when you dip, you receive the likeness of death and burial; you receive the sacrament of that cross – you are then crucified with him; you cling to Christ, you cling to the nail of our Lord Jesus Christ, lest the devil should be able to take you away. Let the nail of Christ hold you, whom the weakness of the human condition recalls (*ibid*. 2.7.23).

The font is a kind of grave, in which the Christian dies and rises again. In baptism 'you laid aside the old age of sin, and took on the youth of grace' (*ibid*. 4.2.7).

For the Fathers, the healing miracles of the Gospels pointed to the spiritual healing accomplished by baptism. 'Christ celebrated this mystery [baptism] in the Gospel as we have read, when he healed the deaf and dumb man' (*De Myst.* 4).

St Ambrose's rite is one of those Western rites in which the ceremony of the '*effeta*' is found. This word is a form of the Aramaic '*ephphatha*' in the story of the healing of the deaf and dumb man (Mk 7.31 f.). In this ceremony the ears and nostrils of the candidate were touched with spittle. Another feature of the Ambrosian rite was the washing of the feet, based on Jn 13. St Ambrose says that hereditary sins are taken away by the washing of the feet, whereas a man's own sins are remitted through baptism. St Ambrose is aware that this practice of foot-washing differs from the Roman rite, but he defends it. This rite is performed following the apostle Peter; it is not merely an example of humility, but brings sanctification.

St Ambrose recalls to the neophytes the ceremonies

they have just undergone, giving a picture of the ceremonies at Milan. After the *effeta,* the candidates en-
tered the baptistery and were anointed. They turned towards the West, renounced the devil and his works, and
the world with its luxuries and pleasures. They were
then exorcised, and the water blessed. The candidates
were baptized by triple immersion with interrogation,
and their heads were anointed with chrism. Then followed the washing of the feet. The newly-baptized each
received a white garment, a symbol of innocence, since
all sins had been cleansed in baptism. The second post-
baptismal anointing makes the baptized a priestly people: 'for we are all anointed with spiritual grace into the
kingdom of God and into the priesthood' (*De Myst.* 30).
Baptism was followed by the eucharist.

Re-baptism

During the third century a serious dispute arose between
the Churches of Africa and the Roman Church about
baptism. We have seen that Tertullian held baptism conferred by heretics to be no baptism at all, and this view
was shared by the Churches of Africa, Asia Minor and
Palestine. In these Churches, a heretic who had been
baptized in heresy and who wished to enter the Catholic
Church had to be 're-baptized'. These Churches did not
believe in a second baptism; heretics were baptized because their first 'baptism' was not a baptism at all. The
Church of Rome held that baptism administered in heresy
could be valid, and she received heretics back into the
Church by a laying on of hands in penance.

The problem of how heretics were to be received back
became a pressing one from the end of the second century onwards. The problem of the validity of a baptism
did not arise in the case of someone who had been baptized as a Catholic and had then fallen into heresy, but

only with regard to someone who had received baptism as a member of a heretical sect. This question came to the fore in the middle of the third century, the protagonists in the debate being St Cyprian of Carthage and Pope St Stephen I.

The Africans held that a heretic could never administer a valid baptism. A heretic, not having the Holy Spirit, could not give it. The validity of baptism would depend in their view on the worthiness of the minister. Pope Stephen held to the traditional position that baptism in the name of the Trinity was valid, even if conferred by a heretic, and that heretics who returned to the Church ought not therefore to be baptized again. Cyprian recognized that Stephen's was the traditional position, but he was convinced that the traditional position was wrong, and he hoped to persuade Stephen to change his views. Cyprian held that there could be no baptism outside the Church. He expounded his views in his treatise *On the Unity of the Church,* which was inspired by the schisms of Felicissimus at Carthage, and Novatian in Rome. Cyprian attacks in strong language the idea that heretics can baptize:

> Whereas there can be only one baptism, they [heretics] think they can baptize; they have forsaken the fountain of life, yet they promise the life and grace of the waters of salvation. Men find there not cleansing but soiling; their sins are not washed away, but only increased. 'New birth' does not bring forth sons to God, but to the devil (*De Unitate,* 11).

Cyprian's position was supported by eighteen Numidian bishops at the Council of Carthage in 255. At the spring Council of 256, eighty-one bishops confirmed this decision, a copy of which was sent to Pope Stephen. The Pope sent a severe letter to Carthage. The breach between the two Churches did not become an open one, since Stephen died in 257, and Dionysius of Alexandria acted as peacemaker between Cyprian and Stephen's suc-

cessor, Pope Sixtus. The debate about baptism was ultimately a debate about the source of authority in the
Church, although Cyprian may not have realized this
fully. St Cyprian died a martyr's death in 257 A.D. The
theological reasoning behind the traditional position up-
held by St Stephen was not worked out or explicitly stated
until the time of St Augustine.

St Augustine

When the Donatist controversy arose in the fourth century, the theological issues underlying the dispute between St Cyprian and Pope St Stephen I had not yet
been pinpointed. The Donatists appealed to St Cyprian
in support of their views about the Church, and it was
left to St Augustine to make a vital distinction which enabled him to solve the problem.

The Donatist movement arose from the aftermath of
Diocletian's persecution, and especially from the conflict
between Christians who had remained faithful during
persecution and those who had lapsed. The movement
took its name from Donatus, the schismatic bishop of
Carthage. The Donatists held that an unworthy minister,
in particular one who had lapsed during persecution,
could not confer a valid sacrament.

The Donatist view of the Church derived from that of
Cyprian. The Catholic Church is one and holy. The
Holy Spirit does not act outside the Church, hence heretic baptism is invalid and does not confer remission of
sins. The Donatists rebaptized Catholics who came over
to their sect. This practice was condemned by two councils. The Council of Arles in 314 A.D. declared that baptism administered in the name of the Trinity was valid,
even though conferred in heresy. The Donatists rejected
the authority of this Council, and were driven to claim
that they alone constituted the true Church.

Augustine solved the problem of heretic baptism by his distinction between the validity and fruitfulness of a sacrament. Heretics have lawful baptism, but they do not have it lawfully (*De Bapt.* 4.7.8). This means that heretics returning to the Catholic Church are not to be rebaptized.

> Let them therefore hasten to the unity and truth of the Catholic Church, not that they may have the sacrament of washing, if they have been already bathed in it, although in heresy, but that they may have it to their health (*ibid.* 5.8.9).

The Donatists confused two ideas by assuming that a baptism which was illicit was also invalid.

For St Cyprian, baptism and the Church were inseparably united to one another, so that baptism could not be conferred outside the Church. Augustine points out that a baptized person can separate himself from the Church without thereby losing his baptism. The objective and indestructible character of baptism derives from the fact that it is Christ (and not the Church) who is the author of baptism. The minister of baptism is Christ's human instrument, and the unworthiness or sinfulness of the minister does not affect the validity of the sacrament, which is conferred by Christ.

> When baptism is given in the words of the Gospel, however great be the perversity of understanding on the part of him through whom, or of him to whom, the sacrament is given, the sacrament itself is holy on account of him whose sacrament it is (*ibid.* 4.12.18).

Augustine's view is the only one which makes the sacramental system intelligible; on the Donatist view it would be impossible to know with certainty whether any sacrament were valid, since the minister might either be a sinner himself, or have been ordained by a sinner.

Augustine's point against the Donatists was that there was no necessary and infallible connection between a sacrament and grace. A sacrament given outside the Church could be valid, without conferring grace. Heretic baptism was therefore valid, although Augustine, like all the Christians of his day, agrees that it did not confer remission of sins. The fruit of the sacrament, remission of sins, could only be obtained when the heretic returned to the Catholic Church. Heretic baptism does not assure the baptized person of participation in eternal life, but it seals his consecration to God, giving him the 'seal of the Lord', i.e. the baptismal character. The idea of baptism as a 'seal' is already found in the second-century Fathers. St Cyprian's mistake, St Augustine pointed out, was his failure to make this distinction between the permanent and unrepeatable effect of the sacrament, and the grace which the sacrament when rightly given and received, confers. Baptism given or received in an unworthy manner is still true baptism, and imprints the character of Christ on the soul. The character is the reason why baptism cannot be repeated. The sacrament will produce its effect of grace when the obstacle preventing this – heresy, schism or a bad disposition – is removed. Thus Augustine was able to show the validity of the traditional view which denied the necessity of 'rebaptizing' baptized heretics.

St Augustine's doctrine of sacramental character is a very important one, which was developed by later scholastic theologians.

Pelagianism

The other great doctrinal controversy in which St Augustine was engaged towards the end of his life, with the Pelagians, led him to develop another aspect of his teaching on baptism. Pelagius and his followers denied the doctrine of original sin, in that they rejected the idea that the sin of Adam had involved the whole human

55

race, and they held that it was at least theoretically possible for man to live without sin. The insistence of Pelagius on both the possibility and the necessity of moral holiness may have looked to St Augustine like a continuation of the Donatist position. Pelagius himself, with his austere moralism, and stress on the autonomy of the human will, was basically pagan rather than Christian, while St Augustine, in the course of his attacks on Pelagianism, lapsed sometimes into a sub-Christian view of God.

In his controversy with Pelagius, St Augustine was driven to stress more and more the reality of original sin, the condition of sinfulness in which the whole of mankind finds itself as a result of Adam's sin. The Church's traditional practice of infant baptism was a key point in Augustine's argument. The Pelagians denied that children were affected by any kind of hereditary sin. St Augustine in reply pointed to the practice of infant baptism. Baptism confers remission of sins; if the Church performs this rite even over infants, it must be that in their case too there is sin which needs to be remitted. In the case of infants, it is not personal sin, but the hereditary sinfulness in which they, like the rest of mankind, are involved. It is this sinfulness, according to St Augustine, which explains both the necessity and the efficacy of infant baptism. Human solidarity in sin explains the need for infant baptism; this same principle of solidarity brings about the child's regeneration in baptism. St Augustine's relentless logic led him to the conclusion that infants who die unbaptized would be damned, although he did add that their damnation would be of the lightest kind. The Pelagians refused to admit that children could undergo punishment for a sin for which they were not personally responsible. They made a distinction between 'the kingdom of heaven' and 'eternal life'; infants who die unbaptized do not enter the kingdom of heaven, but they do have eternal life. A similar distinction to that of the Pelagians had been made by, e.g., St Gregory of Nazianzus (c.329 – 390). Augustine refused to recognize any kind of middle state. The question of limbo will be referred to in the last chapter, but it may be said here that St Augustine's arguments do bring out the difficulties inherent in the thesis of limbo as a state of purely natural happiness. If man is created for God and ordained towards God as his true end, it is hard to see how any form of exile from God's kingdom is to be distinguished from damnation.

A problem that perplexed Augustine was the question of faith in infant baptism. Faith is necessary for baptism, and yet an infant is incapable of making a personal act of faith. When a child was presented for baptism, the priest asked, 'Does he believe in God?' and the sponsors replied, 'He believes' (*Ep.* 98.7). To explain this, St Augustine again made use of the idea of solidarity. As the child has inherited original sin through its carnal procreation by its parents, so it can be freed from original sin by the faith of its parents and sponsors. Their faith expresses the faith of the Church, which supplies for the act of personal faith that is wanting in the child. It is the Holy Spirit who brings about the child's regeneration in baptism:

> For the regenerating Spirit is equally present in the elders offering and in the child offered and reborn; therefore, through this fellowship of one and the same spirit, the will of those offering is useful to the child offered (*Ep* 98.2).

The Holy Spirit can act even where the intention and understanding of the parents is defective, since the children are presented for baptism not merely by their parents and sponsors, but also 'by the whole company of saints and believers'. 'Mother Church who is in the saints does all this because she brings forth wholly all and each' (*Ep.* 98.5).

The child is as yet incapable of exercising faith, and

57

yet it can be said that he believes; he has faith because of the sacrament of faith. St Augustine says that as in a certain manner the sacrament of Christ's body is Christ's body, and the sacrament of Christ's blood is his blood, in the same way the sacrament of faith (baptism) is faith. 'So then, although the child does not yet have that faith which resides in the will of believers, the sacrament of that faith makes him a believer' (*Ep*. 98.10). St Augustine uses the term 'sacrament' in a wider sense than later theologians; it means for him a sacred sign or symbol.

As the child grows up, he must seek to understand this sacrament which he has received, and he will grow in knowledge and love, but even an infant, who understands nothing of what is going on, can receive the sacrament with profit, because of the objective efficacy of the sacrament, which St Augustine is at pains to emphasize. Augustine, in stressing the objective efficacy of the sacrament, is not making the sacrament into something mechanical; underlying and basic to his whole approach is the belief that the sacrament of baptism is a sacrament of faith. The faith of the Church is present where the personal faith of an infant is absent.

CHAPTER 5

BAPTISM IN THE MEDIAEVAL CHURCH

Baptismal practice

Several important changes in the Church's baptismal practice took place during the mediaeval period. The most important of these was the transition from adult to infant baptism as the norm. In the early centuries, the majority of those baptized were adult converts. By about the end of the fifth century, however, most of the candidates for baptism were infants, but the Church continued to preserve for infants the same procedure as for adults; admission to the catechumenate with its various stages, scrutinies, exorcisms, and *redditio symboli,* the ceremony where the candidates (in the case of infants, their sponsors) recited the Creed. In the *Gelasian Sacramentary,* which survived in an eighth-century manuscript, although much of the content is at least two hundred years earlier, the custom of 'scrutinies' on three successive Sundays is preserved. The purpose of the scrutiny was to enquire about the candidate's life and conduct; such ceremonies lost their meaning when applied to infants, yet the Church continued to preserve them. The *Gelasian Sacramentary* also preserves the prayer for the making of a catechumen, the exposition of the Gospels to the 'elect', and the introduction to the Lord's Prayer and Creed. In earlier centuries the distinction between the catechumens and the 'elect' was a real one; a catechumen became one of the elect or chosen when he gave in his name at the beginning of Lent, and was accepted for baptism at the coming Easter. This distinction loses its meaning in the case of infants.

The ceremonies of baptism were gradually compressed, so that the rite of baptism which developed in mediaeval times and was used until recently by the Roman Church, contained the chief stages of the ancient catechumenate, all compressed into one liturgical event. The first part of this ceremony, from the question 'What do you ask of the Church of God?' to the imposition of salt, originally took place on Friday of the third week of Lent. The second part, beginning with the exorcism, originally took place on Wednesday of the fourth week in Lent. The solemn exorcism, *ephphetha,* renunciation of Satan and the anointing took place on the afternoon of Holy Saturday, and the final part of the ceremony took place during the Easter vigil. Thus the Roman rite left us in an unsatisfactory situation, since the rite of an infant baptism was simply a compressed form of the rite for adults. This situation has now been remedied, with the production in 1968 of a new rite of infant baptism, which takes account of the special circumstances of infants. In this rite, greater stress is laid on the role of parents and godparents, and ceremonies such as the exorcisms which were only meaningful in the case of adults are suppressed.

In the early centuries, baptism was normally conferred on the vigils of Easter and Pentecost. The age at which children were baptized varied. Tertullian counselled delay, and Gregory of Nazianzus held that children should not be baptized until about three years of age, when they were old enough to understand something of what was going on. The custom in the West, until the twelfth century, was for children to be baptized on the Easter or Pentecost following their birth. Thus children might be almost a year old at baptism, or only a few days. By the twelfth century, however, bishops and local councils in the West were urging that baptism should take place as soon as possible after birth, since the sacrament of baptism was the only means by which infants could be saved. The influence of St Augustine's doctrine of original sin, together with the high rate of infant mor-

60

tality, made it imperative that infants should be baptized without delay. The occasions on which baptism was administered became more frequent, and Easter and Pentecost lost their special character as seasons for baptism.

Another development which took place in the West was the gradual standardization of baptismal liturgies. In the eighth century Charlemagne ordered the adoption of the Roman rite throughout his empire, and by the twelfth century the Roman rite was in use in all of the Churches of the West, except Milan.

Originally, baptism, confirmation and holy communion were all received in one ceremony, as is still the case in the Eastern Church. In the Roman rite, the post-baptismal anointing by the presbyter was followed by the laying on of hands and consignation by the bishop. When Charlemagne extended the use of the Roman rite throughout his empire, the full rite of Christian initiation could only be conferred in the presence of the bishop; hitherto, in the Gallican rites, presbyters had been able to carry out the whole of the initiation-ceremony.

As a result of Charlemagne's action, baptism was restricted, except in cases where there was danger of death, to the two great feasts of Easter and Pentecost, when the bishop would preside over the administration of baptism in his own church. (Notice how the Masses for the octaves of Easter and Pentecost are full of references to baptism.) In many areas it would be impossible to receive the rite from the bishop himself. This meant that in many cases the baptized would have to wait for their confirmation until the next episcopal visitation. The separation of the two rites of baptism and confirmation began therefore in the eighth century; the reasons for this change were practical rather than theological. In Rome, the Christian rite of initiation retained its primitive unity until the twelfth century.

Since the Fathers viewed the rite of initiation as a unity, they do not make a clear distinction between the effects of the different ceremonies. However, from the time of Tertullian onwards, the laying-on of hands by the bishop was associated with the gift of the Holy Spirit *(De Bapt.* 8). This view was based on the narratives in Acts 8 and 19, where the Holy Spirit is given as a result of the laying-on of hands by the apostles. The Holy Spirit is given in baptism, but the hand-laying by the bishop was seen as bringing a further gift of the Spirit as the completion or perfection of baptism. (For discussion of the meaning of confirmation, see *The Theology of Confirmation* by Paulinus Milner O.P., in this series).

Holy Communion too became separated from baptism. In the later eleventh and early twelfth centuries, with a growing reverence for the consecrated elements (in reaction against Berengar, who appeared to deny the real presence of Christ in the Eucharist,) came doubts as to whether infants could properly receive this sacrament. From the thirteenth century onwards, it became common for adults to receive communion under the form of bread only, and the practice of communicating infants after baptism died out gradually, although it was not finally abolished until the Council of Trent.

There was also during the mediaeval period a change in methods of baptism. The normal practice in the early Church was baptism by total immersion. Baptism by infusion (pouring water on the head) had been used in the early Church only in the case of baptism for the sick, or 'clinical' baptism (from the Greek *kline,* 'bed'). There was a tendency for this kind of baptism to be regarded as less perfect, or even by some Christians, as invalid. If the sick person recovered, he would receive the laying on of hands and signing with chrism from the bishop.

The practice of baptism by immersion continued in the West until about the fourteenth century, but well before this date the practice had become common of baptizing with partial immersion of the body and infusion on the head. Gradually, from the thirteenth century onwards, infusion alone replaced infusion and immersion. The reasons for this change too were practical rather than theological.

Baptism in scholastic theology

The scholastic theologians developed and systematized the teaching of the early Fathers, especially St Augustine. Baptism had been held from the earliest times to be necessary for salvation (cf. Mk 16.16). The early Fathers had therefore held that unbaptized adults could not be saved, except by 'baptism of blood', or martyrdom. The scholastics distinguished between necessity of means and necessity of precept. Baptism was a necessary means to salvation in the case of infants, since, as St Thomas Aquinas said, 'No other remedy is available for them besides the sacrament of baptism' (S.T. 3.68.3). For adults, baptism was both a necessary means and necessary in obedience to Christ's precept, but in their case the lack of baptism could be compensated for by 'baptism of desire'. Adults could be justified by contrition if there was at least an implicit desire for the sacrament. Baptism of desire was commonly held, as by St Thomas, to be desire for the sacrament of baptism as such, although by some theologians it was taken in a wider sense – the desire to do all that is necessary to achieve salvation. The recognition of 'baptism of desire' as a means of salvation where the sacrament itself cannot be had flows from recognition of the principle that 'God is not bound by his sacraments'. The sacraments are the normal means by which the saving activity of God is directed towards men, but the grace of God can reach those who are outside the scope of the Church's visible sacraments. This principle is of vital importance when we come to consider the destiny of the unbaptized, both adults and infants.

The question of validity was much discussed in the mediaeval period. It was recognized that the minister of baptism was not important in himself, but only as an instrument. In cases of emergency baptism could be administered by anyone, even the heretic or unbaptized, provided that the baptizer baptized in the name of the Trinity and had the intention of doing what the Church does; cf. the decree of Pope Nicholas I to the Bulgars, ' "This is he who baptizes" (Jn 1.33), that is, Christ' (Dz 644).

The question of the intention of the minister was discussed as part of the question of validity. It was held by many theologians (Alexander of Hales, Albert the Great, St Thomas) to be the intention to do what the Church does. The right intention in the minister is to be presumed unless there is evidence to the contrary. 'The minister of a sacrament acts in the person of the whole Church, whose minister he is; and in the words which he speaks the intention of the Church is expressed' (S.T. 3.64.8).

Children are to be baptized, although they cannot have personal faith, or the desire to receive the sacrament. From the time of St Augustine onwards, it was generally held that children are saved in baptism by the faith of the Church; St Thomas accordingly bases himself upon St Augustine when he says that children receive salvation 'not through their own act, but through the act of the Church' (S.T. 3.68.9). Since it is the faith of the whole Church which saves the child, the child's salvation is not hindered by the unbelief of his parents. St Thomas stresses, however, that children of Jews and pagans are not to be baptized against the will of their parents; this would be a violation of the natural order.

There was general recognition of the principle that a man cannot be brought into the Church against his will. It was held by the scholastics that a dying man should be baptized if he had previously expressed a desire for it, and that a dying pagan should be baptized if he had not formally refused baptism.

Every baptism validly performed confers the sacramental 'character' on the one baptized, but not every sacrament confers grace. When a man is baptized he normally receives both the character of the sacrament and its effect, which is to produce grace, but the effect of the sacrament can be hindered by the insincerity or bad disposition of the recipient. It is common scholastic teaching, based on St Augustine, that such a man will receive the grace of the sacrament when the '*obex*' or barrier which he has placed in its way is removed. When this bad disposition is removed through the sacrament of penance, the sacrament as it were comes to life and produces its effect, grace. This is known as the 'revivescence' of the sacrament. This name is misleading since it suggests a 'coming to life again', whereas in fact the sacrament 'comes to life' for the first time.

Mediaeval theologians taught that every sacrament confers grace unless the recipient places an *obex* in the way of grace. This is a negative way of expressing the truth. Not to place a barrier means to have the right disposition. Thus, the Council of Florence taught that the sacraments give grace to all who receive them worthily (Dz 1311). It is only for infants that the right disposition consists merely in offering no hindrance to grace.

All the baptized receive equally the 'negative' effects of baptism – the remission of original sin, and in the case of adults of personal sin. St Thomas held that men receive a greater or lesser share in the grace of baptism, depending on the dispositions with which they approach it. Adults have need of the right intention, contrition and faith if the sacrament is to be fruitful, and these dispositions may exist with greater or lesser intensity. Since infants are baptized not in their own faith but in the faith of the Church, St Thomas held that they all receive equally the effects of baptism (S.T. 3.69.8).

The baptized, then, normally receive grace and infused virtues in baptism, as well as the character. The different ways in which adults and infants receive grace and virtues in baptism is explained by St Thomas in terms of the Aristotelian distinction between 'habit' and 'act'. Children are not capable of acts of virtue after baptism, but they receive the habit of faith and virtues through the faith of the Church. This habit or disposition will show itself in acts of virtue as the child grows up. The scholastic doctrine of 'infused faith' as a result of infant baptism develops and explains St Augustine's teaching that children are saved in baptism through the faith of the Church.

St Thomas describes the character given in baptism as a 'share in the priesthood of Christ' (S.T. 3.63.6). It is therefore permanent.

Since the effects of baptism include remission of both original and personal sin, the sacrament of penance is not necessary for an adult before baptism. (If he wishes to go to confession, he may, but his confession is not sacramental.) Concupiscence, or the tendency to sin which remains in man after baptism, is not destroyed, but its power is weakened. The cleansing power of baptism is shown by the symbolism of washing, but the positive effects of the sacrament are equally important. Baptism brings about, through the power of Christ's passion, incorporation into Christ and into the Church, enlightenment, regeneration, the gift of grace and the infused virtues.

Whereas the early Fathers were concerned with celebrating the greatness of the redemption brought about by baptism, the scholastics, while developing the teaching of the Fathers, paid more attention to the external rite: its constituent parts and the conditions necessary for its validity and fruitfulness.

The Protestant Reformers reacted strongly against the scholastic view of the sacraments. They differed from traditional Catholic teaching in rejecting the objective efficacy of the sacraments, expressed in the phrase *ex opere operato* (by the power of the rite itself, i.e. by the power of Christ). Calvin especially stresses that the sacraments are God's instruments, through which he acts as he pleases. To him the Catholic view suggests that the power to justify us and the graces of the Holy Spirit are kept shut up in the sacraments, as though in vessels.

For Luther, the efficacy of the sacrament depends on the faith of the recipient. For Calvin, since faith is only given to the elect, the efficacy of the sacraments depends upon election. The Reformers' insistence upon personal faith creates problems when they come to consider infant baptism. Luther, Zwingli and Calvin all rejected the Anabaptist position, which opposed infant baptism and held baptism performed by an unworthy minister to be invalid.

The second fundamental point on which the Reformers differed from Catholic teaching was with regard to the nature of baptismal regeneration. For the Reformers in general, baptism brought about a change in God's attitude to man; it did not bring about an ontological (as opposed to psychological) change in man himself. Luther held that in baptism sin is not destroyed; God merely ceases to impute to the baptized the sins which remain in his nature after baptism, or to condemn him because of them. He attacked the doctrine, later promulgated by the Council of Trent, that the concupiscence which remains in man after baptism is not itself sin.

A brief survey of the views of three leading Reformers – Luther, Zwingli and Calvin – may bring out the fundamental points of their teaching on baptism.

Luther set forth his baptismal teaching in an early treatise, *The Holy and Blessed Sacrament of Baptism*, written in 1519. Luther stresses throughout that baptism is a sign, and is the work of God, not of men. In baptism God allies himself with man in a 'gracious covenant of comfort' (*op. cit.* 9).

There are three elements, for Luther, in baptism; the sign, the significance and the faith. The sign is the immersion in, and emergence from, the water. The significance is the death to sin and resurrection in the grace of God so that a new man, born in the grace of God, comes forth. However, the dying, or drowning of sin, which baptism signifies, continues throughout the life of the baptized person, and is only completed at death. Sacramentally, the baptized man is guiltless, but because he still lives in sinful flesh, he remains a sinner. The innocence which the baptized person has is so called simply and solely because of the mercy of God.

Luther's views in this treatise were supplemented by his later teaching, especially in the larger and smaller catechisms of 1529 and in his writings against the Anabaptists. In his *Babylonian Captivity* Luther developed his position by saying that a child is regenerated in baptism by infused faith, through the prayer of the Church.

Zwingli

When Zwingli, the Swiss Reformer, wrote his treatise *Of Baptism*, the Anabaptist movement had already broken out in Zurich in 1523. Zwingli defended the traditional practice of infant baptism, without adducing any compelling arguments in its favour. Zwingli based his view on scriptural texts, but his treatment of baptism is considered by many scholars to be thin and unsatisfactory.

For Zwingli, baptism is simply a covenant-sign. External baptism cannot of itself cleanse from sin. Traditional Catholic teaching states that baptism is an *effective* sign, which brings about what it signifies. For Zwingli, however, baptism is an *initiatory* sign, which symbolizes, though it does not effect, an inward change in the baptized person. In Zwingli the separation of sign and thing signified is carried much further than it was by Luther. The covenant-sign of baptism, Zwingli says, pledges the baptized person to a life of faith and discipleship, to the following of Christ. Baptism is considered as a pledge of what Christians ought to do, rather than as a pledge of what God has done for us. Zwingli admits an inherited frailty in our nature, but this is not guilt and does not therefore furnish a reason for infant baptism. Although infants are not capable of having faith, Zwingli defends the traditional practice of infant baptism, since baptism, as a covenant-sign, belongs to the family rather than to the individual.

Like Luther, Zwingli holds that word and sacrament belong together. The word which saves the soul is the word which is inwardly understood and believed.

Calvin

In his *Institutes of the Christian Religion*, published in 1536, Calvin sums up all his theological thought. He combines ideas from both Luther and Zwingli, although he attacks the Zwinglian view that baptism is merely an external sign. Calvin holds that baptism should be received in the light of the promise of Mk 16.16, 'He who believes and is baptized will be saved.'

For Calvin, God's mercy and the pledge of his grace are offered both in his word (the Gospel) and in the sacraments, but he insists that sacraments are secondary and supplementary to the word.

Calvin offers two definitions of a sacrament: 'a sacrament is an outward sign by which God seals on our consciences the promises of his goodwill towards us, to confirm the feebleness of our faith', and 'a sacrament is a testimony of the grace of God towards us, confirmed by an outward sign, with mutual attestation of the piety we bear him' (*Inst.* 4.14.1). These he holds to be similar to St Augustine's definition of a sacrament as 'a visible sign of a sacred thing, or a visible form of the invisible grace'.

Calvin attacks the scholastic view that the sacraments confer grace unless the person to be baptized places an obstacle in the way of grace. 'In promising righteousness without faith, it throws consciences into confusion and damnation' (*Inst.* 4.14.4). In fact, as we have seen, the scholastics did not teach a righteousness apart from faith. They taught that for an adult to receive the sacrament not only validly but fruitfully, he must have some faith and repentance and the desire to receive the sacrament as conferred by the Church.

For Calvin, the sacraments are useful rather than essential. Calvin's stress on the absolute power and majesty of God leads him to reject the idea of any essential relationship between the sacraments and grace, and also enables him to reject the Donatist and Anabaptist view that baptism performed by a wicked minister is invalid.

Baptism for Calvin does not set men free from original sin, but it assures the elect that God's condemnation has been withdrawn from them. Calvin, like Luther, sees the struggle against sin as continuing throughout the believer's life. Romans 7 gives a picture of St Paul's struggle against sin in his regenerate life.

Calvin refutes the Anabaptist rejection of infant baptism by comparing baptism with circumcision. Infants share in the covenant, and cannot therefore be debarred from the covenant-sign. Commenting on Jesus' blessing the children (Mt 19.13-15), he asks why, if infants can be brought to Christ, they cannot also be brought to baptism, the symbol of our fellowship with Christ. Those who bring their children to baptism have confidence because they see the covenant of the Lord signed upon the bodies of their children. The children, too, derive benefit from their baptism, since they are incorporated into the Church.

The Anabaptists asked how infants could be regenerated, since baptism is a sacrament of regeneration and faith. Calvin answers that they are baptized into future repentance and faith, of which 'the seed is planted in them by the secret working of the Holy Spirit' (*Inst.* 4.16.20). This suggests the scholastic doctrine of implicit faith, or faith infused into the child's soul at baptism.

In Catholic thought, the baptism of infants has meaning because of the objective efficacy of the sacrament. An infant, St Augustine pointed out, could receive the sacrament with profit even though personally unaware of what was going on. The Reformers' principle of justification by faith alone (*sola fide*) made it difficult for them to give an intelligible account of what was accomplished in infant baptism. In fact, in retaining infant baptism, (as all the Reformers did, except the Baptists), the Reformers were being inconsistent with their basic principle. If justification is by faith alone, and if faith involves a personal response, it is hard to see how infants can have faith, and how they can be regenerated. These difficulties were pointed out by the Anabaptists, and the leading Reformers did not succeed in answering them in a fully satisfactory way. There was a further problem for the Reformers in retaining infant baptism; scripture was for them the sole rule of faith, and yet infant baptism is nowhere explicitly commended in scripture. It is a practice which rests upon the tradition of the Church.

The *Thirty-Nine Articles* of the Church of England, drawn up in 1571, are based to a large extent on Calvinistic doctrine. The Twenty-Fifth Article, on the sacraments, begins by rejecting the Zwinglian view of sacraments as 'badges or tokens of Christian men's profession', declaring that:

> Rather they be certain sure witnesses and effectual signs of grace, and of God's will towards us, by the which he doth not only quicken, but also strengthen and confirm our faith.

The meaning of this latter part of the statement is ambiguous; it could be taken in a Calvinistic sense, but the statement that the sacraments are 'effectual signs of grace' could be understood as in accordance with the Catholic doctrine about the *ex opere operato* effectiveness of the sacraments.

The Twenty-Seventh Article, on baptism, upholds the reality of baptismal regeneration;

> Baptism is not only a sign of profession and mark of difference whereby Christian men are discerned from others that be not christened, but it is also a sign of regeneration or new birth, whereby, as by an instrument, they that receive baptism rightly are grafted into the Church: the promise of the forgiveness of sins, and of our adoption to be sons of God by the Holy Ghost, are visibly signed and sealed: and grace increased by virtue of prayer unto God.

The Council of Trent

The Council of Trent, in dealing with the sacraments, was concerned to reaffirm the traditional teaching of the Church in opposition to Protestant teaching, rather than to provide new insights. The canons on baptism (Dz

1614-1627) are all couched in a negative form, and directed against specific teachings of the Reformers, especially Luther. By anathematising propositions which are untenable, the Council Fathers make their own position clear.

The Council asserted the truth of the Roman Church's doctrine of baptism in the following terms. It declared that there was a difference between Christian baptism and that of John. For the Reformers there was no difference, since it was faith alone which justified. The objective efficacy of the sacrament was emphasized by the Council's statement that heretic baptism, carried out in the name of the Trinity, with the intention of doing what the Church does, is valid. The Council Fathers declared infant baptism to be necessary for salvation. Baptism once conferred cannot be repeated; there is no question of repeating the sacrament when the child comes to the age of discretion or of deferring baptism until a mature age. A physical washing is necessary in baptism. Those who are baptized can lose the grace of God through serious sin.

In reaction against the Reformers' stress on the importance of the word and of faith, the Council stresses the power of God at work in the sacrament, and the moral obligations that baptism entails.

CHAPTER 6

BAPTISM IN THE CHURCH TODAY

The baptized

In the Dogmatic Constitution on the Church, the Fathers of Vatican II reiterate the teaching of the New Testament and of the Fathers on baptism. The Church, Christ's body, is the setting in which the life of Christ is conveyed to believers through the sacraments. The Council brings out both the Christological and the ecclesial nature of baptism. The work of baptism is to form us to the likeness of Christ. 'In this sacred rite, a union with Christ's death and resurrection is both symbolized and brought about' (*Dogmatic Constitution on the Church,* 7).

Through baptism the faithful share in the priesthood of Christ. 'Through their rebirth and the Holy Spirit's anointing, the baptized receive consecration as a spiritual house, a holy priesthood' (*ibid.* 10). Between the priesthood of the laity and that of the ministry or hierarchy, there is both a difference and a relationship. The priest alone brings about and offers the eucharistic sacrifice, but the people, in virtue of their priesthood, join in the offering of this sacrifice, and exercise their priesthood in their lives as Christians 'by receiving the sacraments, by prayer and thanksgiving, by the witness of a holy life and by self-denial and active charity' (*ibid.* 10).

The baptismal character assigns to the faithful a place in the worship of the Christian religion (*ibid.* 10). Through baptism the faithful are already consecrated to God, so that consecration to God in the religious life is undertaken 'in order to derive more abundant fruit from this baptismal grace' (*ibid.* 44).

Baptism is the basis of the Christian life. It is also the

bond of Christian unity: 'Baptism, therefore, constitutes a sacramental bond of unity linking all who have been reborn by means of it' (*Decree on Ecumenism*, 22). Those who have been validly baptized are joined in some way to the Catholic Church, although they do not enjoy full communion with her (*Dogmatic Constitution on the Church, 15; cf. Decree on Ecumenism, 3*).

The *Ecumenical Directory,* concerned with applying the decisions of Vatican Council II on ecumenical matters, states that a proper value must be placed on the baptism conferred by other Churches and ecclesial communities. The practice of conferring conditional baptism indiscriminately on Christians of other denominations who enter the Catholic Church is not to be approved. Baptism conferred by Eastern Christians is always to be recognized as valid. Baptism by immersion, infusion or aspersion (sprinkling), together with the Trinitarian formula, is of itself valid. In the case of other Christian denominations, what is required for validity is that the minister should have been faithful to the norms of his own community or Church. A baptismal certificate normally suffices to prove this. The right intention (the intention to do what Christians do) is to be presumed in the minister unless there is evidence to the contrary. Conditional baptism is only to be conferred where there is reasonable doubt about either the fact or the validity of the first baptism.

Thus, by recognizing the value and significance of baptism as conferred by other Christian communities, the *Directory* opens the way to dialogue with other Christians about the theology and practice of baptism, a dialogue which is not simply concerned with what is absolutely necessary for the validity of a baptism, but which can enter into discussion about baptism over a wide field.

The *Directory* envisages the possibility of a Catholic acting as godparent at an Orthodox baptism, and vice versa, and in certain cases of Catholics and members of other Christian denominations acting not as godparents but as 'Christian witnesses' at each other's baptismal ceremonies.

The Council ordered the revision of the two baptismal rites for adults, and the rite for infants. The Council made provision also for restoring the different stages of the catechumenate in areas where this is appropriate. Even before the Council, the Congregation of Sacred Rites had given permission in 1962 for the Roman rite of adult baptism to be spread over up to seven stages during the period of preparation for baptism.

Infant baptism

Most of the major Christian denominations today practise infant baptism, a notable exception being the Baptist Church, for whom personal faith is a necessity in a candidate for baptism. Baptists practise 'believers' baptism' when the candidate concerned has reached the stage of desiring to commit himself or herself to Christ through the personal response of faith. However, even in Churches where infant baptism is not practised, there may be a dedication-ceremony at which the child is welcomed into the Church.

In the course of the Church's history, a good deal of discussion has centred on the question of infant baptism. The debate about infant baptism has arisen again in recent years, chiefly as the result of the little book of Karl Barth, originally delivered as a lecture in Switzerland in 1943, and published in English in 1948 as *The Teaching of the Church concerning Baptism*. In this book Barth attacks the practice of infant baptism as 'a wound in the body of the Church'. Barth's approach to the issue of infant baptism or believer's baptism was determined mainly by the historical context; the question was for

77

him the question of the national or the confessing (i.e. anti-Nazi) Church in Germany. We do not want to give up infant baptism, he says, because we do not want to give up the National Church. But baptism in the New Testament is in every case 'the indispensable answer to an unavoidable question, by a man who has come to faith' (p. 42). Baptism requires a personal response, the willingness and readiness of the baptized person to receive the promise of grace which is directed towards him. Barth attacks the Churches' present practice of infant baptism as 'arbitrary and despotic'.

Barth was answered by Oscar Cullmann, whose book *Baptism in the New Testament* was published in English in 1950. Cullman holds that infant baptism is quite compatible with the New Testament doctrine. The foundation of Christian baptism lies in the death and resurrection of Christ, who by his atoning death completed a 'general baptism' for all men. All men therefore in principle received baptism on Good Friday. This baptism is independent of the faith and understanding of those who benefit from it. Baptism as reception into the body of Christ is a divine act, independent of man's action.

The debate about infant baptism was carried on by two more continental scholars, Joachim Jeremias and Kurt Aland, both of whom were concerned with the historical evidence for the practice. Jeremias in *Infant Baptism in the First Four Centuries* (E.T. 1960) recognizes that in the first century A.D. there is no direct evidence of the practice, but he holds that hints may be found in the New Testament itself, especially in the references to the baptism of 'houses' or 'households' (e.g. Acts 11.14; 16.33), which would include children. He also gives reasons for holding that infant baptism developed early rather than late. By the end of the second century, infant baptism is taken for granted.

Aland, in *Did the Early Church Baptize Infants?* (E.T. 1963), questions the arguments of Jeremias, pointing out that there is no direct evidence of infant baptism until the third century.

Jeremias, in *The Origins of Infant Baptism* (E.T. 1963), his reply to Aland, recognizes that there is no direct evidence of infant baptism until Tertullian, but this fact, which is Aland's conclusion, is the starting point for Jeremias, who is concerned to find indirect evidence of the practice in earlier times. A pertinent comment on the whole debate is made by John Frederick Jansen, in his preface to Aland's book: 'Indeed the question of infant baptism is a question of theology. It will not be settled finally by historical demonstration, for it is ultimately a theological question.'

By the third and fourth centuries, the practice of infant baptism is taken for granted in both East and West. We do not know how or by what stages the practice of infant baptism took shape in the early Church, but we know that it is a practice hallowed by the long tradition of the Church. The fact that there is no direct evidence for infant baptism in the New Testament does not, for the Catholic, render the practice invalid. Infant baptism is fully compatible with the New Testament doctrine of baptism, as Cullmann has shown. The incorporation of new members into the Body of Christ, the Church, is the free work of God. It is not man's own act, but the act of God that saves the baptized, so that infants as well as adults can be the objects of God's action. This divine act calls for the response of faith, but man's redemption, which is applied to the individual in baptism, was wrought prior to and independently of the faith of men.

The relationship between faith and baptism is fairly clear in the case of adults (cf. ch. 1). The question of faith in infant baptism was dealt with by St Augustine in terms of the faith of the Church which supplies for the faith of the child, and by the Scholastics, with the doctrine of infused faith. Every baptism involves an act of faith, by the recipient himself if he is an adult, or on the part of the Church if the recipient is a child. As the child grows up, his personal faith will normally come to fruition. The significance of infant baptism is made clearer if the ceremony is performed in the presence of the Christian assembly, so that baptism may be seen to be an act of the Church.

In baptism, a new relationship is created between God and the child; the child becomes a son of God, freed from original sin, but the reality of this relationship depends on the Christian education of the child. This is why a priest may refuse to baptize a child if there is no likelihood of his receiving a Christian upbringing. In this case the sacrament would not bear fruit. However, a child in danger of death may be baptized.

Baptism, then, brings about a real change in the child, an ontological change on which the child's future spiritual development depends. The parents and sponsors of the child have the great responsibility of helping the child as it grows up to grow into a personal awareness and acceptance of the saving relationship with God opened up to him by baptism. The whole of the Christian life may be seen as a gradual appropriation of the new dimension of life and of the saving grace freely bestowed upon the individual by God in baptism.

The unbaptized

1. Adults It has long been recognized in the Church that 'baptism of blood' (martyrdom) can replace the Church's sacrament of baptism as a means of bringing men into the kingdom of God and eternal life. In mediaeval thought another means of salvation was recognized: 'baptism of desire'. If we are to affirm both that 'God desires all men to be saved, and to come to the knowledge of the truth', and that 'there is one mediator between God and men, the man Christ Jesus' (1 Tim

2.4-5), we must clearly hold that there is a means of salvation for those who are outside the scope of the Church's visible sacraments. This is an important principle for us today, with our knowledge that many people, even in Christian countries, have never been effectively presented with the Gospel.

'Baptism of desire' does not necessarily mean 'desire for baptism'. It has become a technical term of theology, denoting the way in which men of good will are linked to the Church, men who, if they knew about the sacrament of baptism, would desire it. Desire for baptism, or for God, may not be explicitly expressed, but any movement towards the good is in fact a movement towards God, whether a man is conscious of the fact or not. Any devotion to a worthy cause, such as justice or truth, may be implicitly devotion to God. In order to be saved, a man must have love for God, although he may not know that it is in fact God whom he loves (cf. Mt 25.31-45, the parable of the sheep and the goats). A true love for others involves a going out from oneself, a death to self, through which the one who loves shares, often without realizing it, in the death and resurrection of Jesus, and is reborn to a new life for others. Such a disposition of love predisposes a man to receive grace. But baptism of desire, like the sacrament of baptism, is not obtained by purely human activity; it is always a response to the initiative taken by the grace of God. This death to self is not achieved by one's own efforts, but is a gift of God.

If a man's life is orientated towards God, even if only implicitly, then he is living in a state of grace. St Thomas Aquinas taught that when a man arrives at the age of reason,

> the first thing to which his thought must then turn is to deliberate about himself. And if he directs himself towards the true end, he receives grace and the remission of original sin (S.T. 1a 2ae 89.6).

81

This directing of oneself towards the true end need not be something accomplished once for all in a single act; it might well be applied to the whole aim and direction of a man's striving throughout his life.

Some theologians have put forward the hypothesis of a 'final choice' at the moment of death. According to this view, all men may be given the opportunity at the moment of death to make a definitive personal choice, either for God or against him. Such a final choice would of course normally be the expression of the general tendency of a man's life up to that point. This hypothesis springs from a concern to show that in some way salvation is genuinely offered to all men.

Baptism of desire cleanses from original sin and remits personal sin, but it does not confer the character, nor does it bring about incorporation into the visible Church. Those who are joined to Christ and to the Church by baptism of desire do not therefore enjoy the benefits of the sacramental and liturgical life of the Church, but they are partakers of salvation, which is not confined to members of the institutional Church. This latter point was strongly asserted in a letter sent by the Holy See to Cardinal Cushing in 1949 (Dz 3866). It is, however, only through actual incorporation into the visible Church that men can share fully in all the blessings of salvation which are received by members of the Church as a worshipping community.

2. *Infants*   What happens to children who die unbaptized before reaching the age of reason? This has often been a very real and agonizing problem for Christians. It is not a question that is clearly answered by revelation, but theologians at various periods in the Church's history have reached out for possible answers.

St Augustine, in opposition to Pelagius, taught that children dying unbaptized suffer the pains of hell, though in a mitigated form. In saying this, Augustine

82

was striving to maintain the necessity of grace for salvation and the gratuitousness of God's gifts. Augustine's position was modified by Anselm and the later Scholastics, who said that such children go not to hell but to limbo. The doctrine of limbo, first put forward by Anselm (d. 1109), was only elaborated in the thirteenth century, and although it has been and is widely held, it has never been formally defined by the Church. Limbo has been variously described at different times in the Church's history, and ideas of limbo have become progressively milder. Limbo is generally described now as a state where such children are deprived of the beatific vision, but enjoy a purely natural happiness.

The question of limbo has been much discussed by Catholic theologians in recent years, and an increasing number of modern scholars are questioning the theory of limbo as it has been traditionally understood. To say that children who have not been baptized, through no fault of their own, are deprived of the vision of God for all eternity seems to many people to compromise either the omnipotence or the love of God.

There is also a difficulty involved in the concept of limbo as a state of 'purely natural happiness'. There is in fact no such thing as a 'purely natural man'. This term is an abstraction; it does not represent the actual state of any individual man. Because of the redemption, all men are potentially 'graced'. All men have an innate yearning for God; they are so made as to find their happiness only in him. Therefore talk of a 'purely natural happiness' seems almost a contradiction in terms; unless the children in limbo remain in a permanent state of infancy, how can they enjoy happiness while being separated from the presence of God in whom alone true happiness is to be found?

Those who question the thesis of limbo do not dispute the doctrine of original sin or the fact that it is impossible for any one to enter heaven in a state of original sin.

They consider the possibility that there may be some means by which original sin can be remitted, other than the sacrament of baptism. For a child to die unbaptized may not necessarily mean that the child dies in a state of original sin.

Some form of baptism – either sacramental baptism or baptism of desire – is universally recognized by Catholics as necessary for salvation. It is also universally recognized that God is not bound by the sacramental order he has instituted. Various theories have been put forward by Catholic scholars to explain how, in the case of unbaptized infants, baptism of desire could be regarded as realized. Cajetan had taught that the desire of the parents supplied for the baptism lacking in their child who had died. This theory was discussed at the Council of Trent and was not formally condemned. Others have regarded the faith of the Church as supplying for the faith of the unbaptized, as well as of the baptized child. Some modern theologians such as Boros have thought in terms of a choice at the moment of death by which even an infant might attain to the use of reason and be enabled to make an act of love for God, and so enter heaven. At the moment of death children would arrive at spiritual maturity and be enabled to make a choice for God.

An attempt has been made to discuss the fate of unbaptized children, not in terms of a choice at the moment of death, but from a consideration of the nature of redemption. Vincent Wilkin S.J. in *From Limbo to Heaven* points out that the exclusion of unbaptized children from the beatific vision compromises the compassion of Christ and the power of God. These infants embody the state of the race as a whole; they typify the condition of man, which is a condition or state of original sin, of alienation from God. These children are born into a world which is alienated from God, although they have not personally chosen to reject God and to continue in this state of alienation. Christ, by his death and resurrection,

has redeemed the whole of mankind. This process of redemption is still mounting towards its climax, but when
the climax is reached, death, which is the penalty for
original sin, will be abolished. Wilkin questions whether
children, who embody in themselves the condition of the
totality of men, can be said to continue in a state of original sin when original sin itself, as a state of racial re-
volt and enmity towards God, has been abolished. The
state of being 'in Adam' will no longer exist at the Last
Day (except for those who have chosen to reject God).
By their death and resurrection, or rebirth, on the
Last Day, these children will no longer embody the state
of the sinful human race, but of the human race as redeemed, indwelt by the Holy Spirit, and established for
ever in the grace and favour of God. As members of the
redeemed race, they will be born into the grace of Christ
without a personal act, as they are born into original sin
without a personal act. They now embody the state of
the redeemed human race. In other words, these unbaptized infants are saved in a corporate way, by undergoing a universal 'baptism' which takes place on the Last
Day. Wilkin's approach is an attempt to see how unbaptized children might be saved, using the insights of Pau-
line theology.

Peter Gumpel, S.J. has written two articles in the
Downside Review on this question (see Bibliography).
Gumpel's thesis, which is fully documented, is that the
traditional view – that infants who die without baptism
are excluded from the beatific vision – is not theologically
certain. Gumpel does not set out to discuss the merits
of alternative theories, but merely to show that, since the
relevant pronouncements of Church authorities do not
decide the question definitively, doubts about the traditional position can legitimately be expressed.

Pope Pius XII in an address to midwives on 29 Octo-
ber 1951 stressed the need for baptizing babies in danger of death. He did not state categorically that there is

no possibility of salvation for unbaptized children. The question of the destiny of unbaptized children remains an open one; the only answer we can give to this question is that we do not know. But by building on facts that we do know – that Christ by his death and resurrection has effected in principle the salvation of all mankind and that God's grace is not confined to the sacraments, a number of modern theologians have developed the doctrine of limbo further along the lines of its original purpose and have indicated that, although we do not know how God will act in such a case, we may surely trust in his mercy and in his universal salvific will with regard to these children. Such children may be entrusted to his infinite power and love, which are not limited by human circumstances.

This newer approach to the problem does not lessen either the need for or the value of baptism. God may give grace to children before reception of the sacraments, as he does to adults who receive baptism of desire, but such a pre-sacramental bestowal of grace does not make the reception of the sacrament unnecessary or meaningless. Similarly with infants, if God does give grace where the sacrament itself cannot be received, the sacrament remains necessary in cases where there is a possibility of receiving it.

EPILOGUE

We have looked briefly at the ways in which baptism has been understood by theologians in different periods of the Church's history; we must also consider what it means for us, as twentieth century Christians.

We have seen that in the New Testament, and throughout the Church's history, the theology of baptism has had both a Christological and ecclesiological aspect. The Christological dimension of baptism is expressed by the old English word 'christening'. It is made clearer by the modern trend towards understanding the sacraments in personal rather than physical categories (see e.g. E. Schillebeeckx, *Christ the Sacrament*). Each sacrament is an encounter with Christ, the risen Lord; baptism is the sacrament which makes such encounter possible, by bringing about a relationship between Christ and the baptized. Baptism brings about fellowship with Christ and opens up a relationship in which, through freely given obedience, the baptized person lives with Christ's own life and grows gradually into full human maturity. This relationship demands that we make Christ, and not ourselves, the centre of our lives.

The life which we receive in baptism is the life of the Blessed Trinity, the life of the three Divine Persons indwelling us in the very depths of our being. Thus we share in the life of God himself; we receive the Spirit of adoption, who makes us sons of the Father in Christ. For the Jews, God was present in the Jerusalem Temple; but since the coming of Christ, every Christian is himself the temple or sanctuary of God (1 Cor 3.16). He is therefore holy, that is, consecrated or set apart for God. Thus the baptized Christian, as a living temple, is one of the means by which God is present to men.

This presence of the Blessed Trinity in us is the basis of our life of prayer. It is Christ in us who prays to the Father, and we unite ourselves to the prayer of Christ. St Paul tells us that the Spirit intercedes for the 'saints', that is, for all Christians. It is through the Spirit that God communicates to men the gift of his life and of his transforming presence.

This new life will show itself in obedience to Christ, an inner spontaneous obedience to the Holy Spirit who indwells the believer. This obedience brings about true freedom, liberation from the narrowness of selfishness. 'You will know the truth, and the truth will make you free' (Jn. 8.32). We are empowered to act in this way because in baptism our very being has been transformed. Through baptism, the fulfilment of Jeremiah's prophecy is achieved:

> But this is the covenant which I will make with the house of Israel, says the Lord: I will put my law within them, and I will write it upon their hearts; and I will be their God, and they shall be my people. And no longer shall each man teach his neighbour and each his brother, saying, 'Know the Lord'; for they shall all know me, from the least of them to the greatest, says the Lord (Jer 31.31-34).

To know God in Hebrew thought means not merely an intellectual knowledge but an experiential knowledge. This knowledge of God, in the sense of an intimate relationship, is brought about in baptism, and this is the reality which is described by the term 'grace'.

Baptism also introduces the baptized person into the Church, and into the Church's life as expressed in worship. The ecclesial dimension of baptism is made more evident when a baptism takes place in the presence of the local church, so that the Christian assembly can pray for and welcome its new member.

Baptism, then, introduces the baptized into the life of Christian worship, and gives him a part to play in the

Church's liturgy. By baptism Christians share in the priesthood of Christ, and in union with the ministerial priesthood they offer the Eucharistic sacrifice to God, offering him also their own lives for his service. The recent liturgical changes have emphasized the role of the laity in public worship, and have brought to the fore the biblical concept of the priesthood of the laity.

Baptism is seen in the New Testament as a consecration to God, making the baptized a priestly people. Christians are called 'to be a holy priesthood, to offer spiritual sacrifices acceptable to God through Jesus Christ' (1 Pet 2.5). Later in the same chapter the writer speaks of Christians as 'a chosen race, a royal priesthood, a holy nation, God's own people' (1 Pet 2.9). Christians, then, share in the priesthood of Christ, not in the full sense in which the ordained priest does, but still in a very real sense. This priestly vocation is one aspect of the mission confided to Christians by their baptism.

Baptism ought not to be seen as something accomplished once for all, as a ceremony which for most Christians happened in childhood. It is rather the beginning of a process:

> Baptism itself is only a beginning, a point of departure, for it is wholly directed towards the acquiring of fulness of life in Christ. Baptism is thus oriented toward a complete profession of faith, a complete incorporation into the system of salvation such as Christ himself willed it to be, and finally toward a complete participation in Eucharistic communion (*Decree on Ecumenism*, 22).

Baptism is the foundation on which the whole Christian life rests; it is the gateway to the other sacraments. It is the beginning of a process of growth into the likeness of the risen and glorified Christ, a process which will reach its final consummation only at the Last Day.

Baptism as consecration to God also implies and involves a consecration to the service of one's fellow men, since these two aspects of the Christian vocation cannot be separated. Baptism is thus a call to share in Christ's work of redeeming the world. The Christian is called to holiness, to a life conformed to that of his master. He must live according to the grace he has received. The Christian vocation given in baptism also directs our attention outwards to the needs of the world. The social encyclicals of recent Popes have called on all Christians and all men of goodwill to work for social justice. Our own age is particularly conscious of the Christian vocation to service, for example among the socially deprived or the less developed nations. Each Christian is called by baptism to serve his fellow men, according to his circumstances, by prayer and action on their behalf. The love which the Christian shows to others is a reflection of and bears witness to the primordial love of God, which is poured out upon Christians in their baptism. Baptism is a sign of God's love; it is also an eschatological sign, pointing forward to the final consummation when the process of salvation, initiated by baptism, will reach its fulfilment.

And he who sat upon the throne said, 'Behold, I make all things new.' Also he said, 'Write this, for these words are trustworthy and true.' And he said to me, 'It is done! I am the Alpha and the Omega, the beginning and the end. To the thirsty I will give water without price from the fountain of the water of life. He who conquers shall have this heritage, and I will be his God, and he shall be my son' (Apoc 21.5-7).

BIBLIOGRAPHY

General: Article 'Baptism' in *Sacramentum Mundi,* Vol. 1, ed. K. Rahner, C. Ernst and K. Smyth, Burns and Oates 1968.

B. Neunheuser O.S.B.: *Baptism and Confirmation,* Herder – Burns and Oates, 1964. Survey of these two sacraments from the New Testament to the present day.

E. C. Whitaker: *Documents of the Baptismal Liturgy,* S.P.C.K., 1960. Translation of about forty passages relating to baptism in East and West, up to the ninth century.

On Chapter 1:

W. F. Flemington: *The New Testament Doctrine of Baptism,* S.P.C.K., 1957. A survey of the New Testament evidence by an Anglican scholar.

R. Schnackenburg: *Baptism in the Thought of St Paul,* B. Blackwell, 1964.

On Chapters 2 and 3:

J. Daniélou S.J.: *The Bible and the Liturgy,* Notre Dame Press, 1964. Chapters 1 to 6 are a study of the typology of baptism in the early Fathers.

On Chapter 5:

J. D. C. Fisher: *Christian Initiation: Baptism in the Mediaeval West,* S.P.C.K., 1965. A study of the rite of Christian initiation and its gradual breaking up into its component parts.

On Chapter 6:

Adult Baptism and Initiation, in *Concilium* Vol. 2, No. 3, Feb. 1967.

P. Gumpel S.J. 'Unbaptized Infants – May They be Saved?' in *Downside Review,* Vol. 72, 1953–4, pp. 342-458, and 'Unbaptized Infants – A Further Report', *Downside Review,* Vol. 73, 1954–5, pp. 317-346.

INDEX

THEOLOGY TODAY SERIES

The following numbers *have already been published:*